Tales From The Parking Lot

Denny Sieber

To order additional copies of this book, contact:
Xlibris Corporation
1-888-795-4274
www.Xlibris.com
Orders@Xlibris.com
108556

Tales From The Parking Lot

CONTENTS

FORWARD

This is a collection of tales about nature, fishing, adventure, humor, history, and dumb teenage acts. All is true, at least as I remember things.

Don't expect the Great American Novel, or for that matter a true biography. You'll find out a lot about me as it is, as you read. This is necessary to help you understand where these tales are coming from. I'm not sure myself, but I had a lot of fun living these tales.

I've never had any formal education past high school. I never read but a half dozen books in my life until my mid-fifties, when, on a Montana trip, friends Reed and Jim and I stopped at Wall City, SD. They bought a pile of books about Indians and mountain men. I thought to myself, what a waste of time and money. Well, with the hundreds of miles we drove, I was often in the back of the truck in a built-in bunk, and bored. Eventually, I picked up a book and started to read. Soon I was hooked and even now, in my late 70's, I read from three to six books a month. As long as the author tells a good story, I enjoy them. A few years ago, Walt Young's *Pennsylvania Outdoor Times* offered readers a chance to enter short stories. Because this started during hunting season, and I knew the editor, I thought I'd try it. Sure enough, it got published, which gave me enough confidence to try to tell some more stories, which need to be told rather than be buried with me. My kids and grandchildren will be mortified at some of the things I did and the time I wasted doing them. Sorry—what I am is what you get.

CHAPTER ONE—THE EARLY YEARS

I was born in January of 1933, near the end of the Great Depression, the youngest of five with three brothers and one sister. We were poor, but I thought we were middle class, just like everyone else in our neighborhood. Below our back yard was a ball field and a small creek beyond that. Every house had kids who would meet there most evenings, and most of the adults too. Horseshoes, marbles, ball games, track meets, and whatever else our imaginations could dream up took place. One kid became the state marbles champ.

I was naturally drawn to the water and wanted to fish, although I had no idea how to go about it. Finally, my brother Bob made me a rod by straightening out a wire clothes hanger, bending an eye on the end, and putting it in a piece of broom handle, then an empty thread spool on a nail for a reel, and a bent pin for a hook. The bait I could handle myself, as our back yard was mostly vegetable garden. It didn't take long to gather several worms, which went into a Prince Albert tobacco can. After many trips and lots of advice, I finally caught a few 2-3" minnows. A monster was turned loose! I was 4 or 5 years old at the time.

Fortunately, I got to playing ball and doing other things, like building "shacks," catching garter snakes, and making swimming holes in that 5-6' stream. Mom always said I should have been born with fins and gills.

I especially remember our first big track meet. It was a sign to me that I was really growing up and could do some things as well or better than the big kids. In my pre-teen years, I never walked anywhere—I *ran*. If it was two blocks to the neighborhood store—I ran. If I went to the ball field—I ran. My friend's house—I ran. Well, you get the idea.

For our track meets, we cut saplings in the nearby woods for pole vaulting; we used a fairly round stone for shot puts and a fairly flat stone for discus, saw horses for hurdles, and for finish lines we just scratched a line in the dirt.

We had one super athlete a tad older than me. John S. could pole vault onto his garage roof and land on his feet at the age of 12. He was a fast runner and a good ball player too. However, John was a bit odd. He never went out for sports in high school and spent his adult years in the Army. He would also sit on top of their chicken coop and announce imaginary baseball games (including crowd noise) for hours. My mother would just howl and laugh when John's voice came across the hollow.

I entered everything, but didn't do well until our "marathon"—twice around the ball field, then the length of our alley, which was two blocks, then the upper alley, another two blocks, then the length of our street, yet another two blocks. I was having fun trotting along watching all the kids my age drop out, then most of the older kids. When we started down the final block of our street, it was just me and two senior high boys. I was wondering when they would leave me in the dust, but then realized they were gasping for breath, so I ran as fast as I could and beat them by half a block! Bubbling with joy, I accepted congratulations and pats on the back, but I knew better than to strut or brag because they could still whip my skinny little butt.

Zook's Dam

I had a great summer vacation one year when I got to visit my cousin Willis at our grandparents' farm in Juniata County. Will and his younger brothers, Irving and Curtis, were staying there with their mother that summer during World War II. His dad was in the Panama Canal zone working with heavy equipment to widen the canal. We had a great time driving everyone batty with our energy and noise. They let us clean out a chicken coop for a club house and we actually did a pretty good job for a 10—and 11-year-old. We even painted it unintentionally. We had made about ten bottles of "ink" from inkberry bushes. We gathered the bottles from the dump, mostly medicine bottles, filled them with inkberry juice and capped them tightly. Later when we visited again, I asked Will if he had been up to the clubhouse. He said "No" so we went up. The whole inside was covered in purple polka dots. Grandma, Grandpa, Willis' mom (Aunt Bessie) and my mom got a big laugh. Apparently the "ink" had fermented and exploded.

Anyhow, to get rid of Willis and me, Aunt Bessie would take us to Zook's Dam to fish. Amazingly, at our young age, she left us there and picked us up late afternoon. We had our sticks with stringed hooks, plus worms. We not only didn't drown or get in any trouble, but sat in boats that were tied up and proceeded to catch a batch of really nice bluegills. Aunt Bessie came back on time and was very surprised with our catch. She not only praised us but cleaned and fried the fish. It fed us, and our grandparents and Irving. (Curt was a baby then.) It was the first time I ate fish and really enjoyed it.

That was the real start to my addiction to fishing. We never got back to the dam for years, however. Later the dam was breeched and it dried up except for Licking Creek, which fed it, and a small lily pad pond.

CHAPTER TWO—JESS

As I reached my pre-teen and early teen years, we were allowed to go a little farther from home, with much begging and pleading to our parents. Before that, when we got caught, my Mom's favorite punishment of choice was her potstick, a wooden paddle about two feet long. She didn't have to use it much because we had lots to do near home.

Goss' Dam, located on Jack's Creek, was the nearest place to swim in those days. Many families would go there—no beach, no lifeguards, cold water—but we loved it. The family that lived there had a little store like a concession stand when they had enough customers. People would go there and have picnic lunches and spend the day. It was only 2-3 miles away, but we drove the old Model T. Later we moved a bit farther into town and my new friend Jess and I walked there often, never thinking about how far it was.

That was when we both started fishing a bit more seriously. It started with sticks and string with real hooks. Soon we had telescope rods and casting reels, when we could afford them—or hand-me-downs. The equipment ballooned out of control after we got older and began to earn money, but that's another story, and one many fishermen and hunters have experienced.

There was a man who lived near there who fished the dam and often talked to us. He had a crippled arm from WWII and he'd made a holster for the rod to fit in mounted on his belt. He had the first spinning rod I ever saw and we were fascinated by it. I don't remember if monofilament line was made then or not, but it was about that time.

Anyhow, we occasionally caught some rock bass and other pan fish—enough to whet our appetite but not enough to cook any—yet. On our way home we'd often take a short cut through fields. Several times we'd harvest some potatoes and eat them raw. After all, we'd been away since early morning and of course didn't pack a lunch. One time there was a rotting carcass of a cow in the field. I lost my appetite soon that day, but Jess had to sink a couple arrows into it with his homemade bow and arrows. Sometimes I wondered about him.

My new friend Jess and I just had to try all the fishing we could get to. We pestered our parents and Jess' Dad often took us, as well as my parents. "Old Jess" often fished with us, and usually had some sunshine beer with him or muscatel wine. Oddly it didn't seem to affect his driving, although he might have gone a little slower. I never saw the '37 Plymouth weave, nor did he make any stupid decisions. Thank God! Only once were we concerned.

That time we were on the Juniata River in the summer time and young Jess and I had gone about a mile downstream, when a hard thunderstorm struck. We went to the highway and trudged back to the car. No Jess Sr. Jess Jr. said, "I bet he had a bottle hid in the car," so we went to the river and thankfully, "old Jess" was sitting on a rock with his two rods propped on sticks, "still fishing" and watching his rods closely when we came to him. Jess Jr. said, "Jess, (he called his dad by that) what are you doing?" It was still pouring *hard!* Jess Sr. turned to us and said, with his eyes like two black marbles, "I'm fishing, what the H—do you think I'm doing?" As if the sun was shining and the birds were tweeting.

Well, we gave him several hours more to fish, and when we went home, he drove a bit slower, but safely.

Often we'd go fishing for suckers and catfish in the winter, and another older bachelor would go along too. He didn't drive, but he was a good cook and would usually bring some goodies along. Jess and I seldom brought food, but we didn't have any qualms about eating his, especially if he had baked a pie or a cake.

"Fat," his nickname aptly, would usually bring a jug of gasoline along to start a fire with, both to keep warm and to see when fishing at night. He loved to throw the remainder of the gas in the fire when Jess and I were half asleep, then yell and warn us so we'd be fifty feet or more away when it blew up. The flame would shoot twenty-five or more feet high. Try running half asleep, along the river in the dark.

One winter night, Fat caught and kept several walleyes, which they called "Susquehanna salmon" then. I had never seen one before and didn't know if it was legal or not, but it didn't matter to Fat.

We also burned old tires and they'd make a smoky stinky mess and we'd choke on the fumes. So, if we had time before dark, Jess and I would hunt up a nice pile of firewood if it was dry enough. Once we got some pieces of old railroad ties, which stunk as bad as the tires.

Even though Fat made good money at the steel mill and lived with his sister, he went through money like it was water. Jess and I saved every penny we could, gathered pop bottles for the deposit money and even did some odd jobs, plus our small allowances from our folks. Often, Fat would be broke before payday and we could get some great buys on his fishing equipment. Once I got a pair of "Wonder Rods" for $10.00 each. I saved hard and long to get them. I already had a pair of Pflueger casting reels.

My Dad and Mom would usually eat any fish I got: suckers, catfish, whatever. Later, when we caught so many big fall fish in Tuscarora creek, Dad said no more of them.

One bitter cold January, I was 14 or 15 and had a severe case of cabin fever. Mom and Dad were going to Juniata County that day and wondered if I wanted to go along. I said yes—as far as Lost Creek. They thought I was loony but dropped me off and picked me up four or five hours later. My line kept freezing in the guides and I didn't catch a thing. The temperature got to 2 degrees F that day, but I convinced myself I had a great day.

Our trips to Strodes Run in the spring was next in our education. We would fish the mouth of the stream where it went into the Juniata River for suckers, and caught several trout too, so we talked our parents into taking us there in April-May. We caught a few trout, but had trouble keeping from "still fishing" with rod props, etc. We had no one to teach us how to drift the bait naturally, yet.

There was a privately owned dam on the the stream at that time, with signs to keep out. We fished above and below the property until one day when Jess couldn't resist. There were no cars at the summer house. He waded as far as he could at their beach, and with a solid glass fly rod and a big night crawler, he heaved it out as far as he could. Soon a car pulled up and the owner said, "Get out, kid, this is private property." Well, Jess pulled up his chain stringer with a 17" and a 19" brown trout on it. The man was so dumbstruck all he could say was" . . . and stay out!"

Another day, we were at the upper end just on the legal side of the Keep Out signs. A guest of the owner on the lake side had hooked onto a big "hog," but was so inept that he broke an expensive cane rod into several pieces and lost the trout. The man was obviously upset, but only complained to us about the cost of the rod. We were sympathetic with him, but later had a good laugh about how bad a fisherman he was.

One time we went to Strodes Run with some food, which we ate as soon as my mom left. However, we had a jug of orange Kool-Ade chilling in the stream, which we rationed because it was hot. It wasn't long before two girls about our same age came along. They started pestering us for the Kool-Ade and being annoying in general. We ignored them until they grabbed the jug and ran off with it. Jess got the jug back from the one girl, but the other had the lid. I chased her down into the brush and wrestled with her, and finally found the lid in her front pocket. I brought the lid back and put it on the jug, while Jess was trying to keep the other girl from getting it again. Finally they left in disgust.

Later, after not catching any more fish, I said to Jess, "You know, they weren't bad looking." Jess said, "I was just thinking the same thing." Then we both laughed.

That summer we got Mom to take us back to Strodes Run again. This time we had the latest solid glass rods and Bach-Brown spinning rods. Mono line still wasn't available, but the lures and weights we used were heavy enough that we didn't need mono line.

It was very hot, so once we waded down river some distance, near where the creek flowed into the river, we decided to fish in the buff, except for sneakers. We caught some nice small mouth, plus big rock bass, and enjoyed the wading—up to our necks sometimes. Didn't see another human all day. That's how it often was in the 40's and early 50's. We finally got back to the gravelly sand bar with weeds on it, and began to dress. Jess picked up his white undershorts and let out a loud shriek. (I won't say scream.) A huge water snake dropped down from the shorts and landed between us. After our nerves settled, we shook out every piece of clothing before putting them on. Jess' Mom wondered how his undershorts had brown in them. I don't think she believed the true story.

The next year we both got identical fly rods from Montgomery Ward, and we began to fish a small mountain stream called Licking Creek. Our rods were made the same way the Shakespeare Wonder Rods were, except ours were yellow rather than white. We were tough, hard-nosed kids and didn't think too much about fishing all day, and doing it through tough walking through heavy brush, thickets, etc., until Jess's Dad (Jess, Sr.) dropped us off and went 5 or 6 miles upstream instead of half way. We were a couple of tired puppies that day when we got home.

Around this time I began to realize Jess almost always caught more fish than I did, even though we fished together with identical equipment. I couldn't figure it out, and attributed it to luck, because I did as well as he did with pickerel and fall fish, which we got from Tuscarora Creek. Then one day on Tuscarora, I watched Jess fish through a deep riffle I had just fished without results, and he got two nice small mouth bass about 15". He explained that he drifted the bait naturally through the chute just like for trout, but deeper than I did. Sometimes I almost have to be hit on the head to see things. I still wouldn't admit for a long time that he was much better than I was with trout, because I held my own with other guys our age. One day on the way home from a trout trip, he was rubbing it in, and I said, "Man, are you cocky." Jess replied, "It's not cocky if you can do it." That about sums it up. Since he's no longer with us, I'll do some bragging for him.

About that same time period, Jess went to the camp we had access to on Tuscarora Creek. I couldn't go that day. He called me at home later and said, "Come on up and see what I got today." "Okay, I'll be be up soon." Twenty minutes later, I saw the biggest crappie I ever hope to see. It was 19 ½" and covered a large meat platter completely. I don't know what it weighed because they never checked it out with the Fish Commission—they ate it! He'd caught it in the "crappie hole" above Pomeroy's Dam, just some brush snagged in some hedge apple trees (orange osage.) We often caught some there, but seldom over 12" and never over 13".

We called fall fish "poor man's trout" and would use helgramites for them, also for bass, bluegills, rock bass—anything that would eat them. Jess got a fall fish that was 19 ½" once, below Pomeroy's Dam. My biggest was 17 ½," but we caught many around 15".

In later years, on a first day of trout season on Penn's Creek, I saw Jess with one of his daughters. It was a beautiful day, but the water was very cold and few fish were being caught, none by me and the people who were with me. I yelled to Jess on the other side of Penn's "How are you doing?" "Not too bad. I got my limit, (8 per day back then) and need two more for my daughter." He then said, "We got to get going because I'm playing golf this afternoon." I read the next Monday in the local paper that he got a hole-in-one. And so it goes. He was a good hunter too. The first time he went for deer, he shot a 6 point buck with a "punkin ball" and a shotgun. I understand he was a good turkey hunter also, later on.

Back to when we were kids, as we started trout fishing and spending time on Tuscarora Creek, we figured we were too old to play marbles any more. Jess' younger brother, John, had confiscated many of Jess' marbles, but with what he had and my huge bag, we took them to the local cemetery that overlooked town. No, we didn't bury them. We took my Babe Ruth model baseball bat along. By the way, the only new, unrepaired bats were owned by rich kids. We got ours by bumming bats that had been broken in adult league games. Then, with glue, screws, and tape, they were as good as new.

Do have any idea how far you can hit a marble with an oversized Babe Ruth model baseball bat? We didn't know either, except for weak foul balls that went anywhere from 100 yards to out of sight. Even though we hit them toward town, we never heard of anyone getting hurt or windows broken. It was a dumb thing to do, but it was fun, though tiring. Try driving 700 to 1,000 balls into the outfield and it'll give you an idea how tired. There may have been 2,000 marbles.

As I mentioned before, there was a crappie hole in Tuscarora Creek. It was a good one for small minnows and a bobber, but it was only the size of about a 9' by 14' room. I remember one spring a bunch of men from

a nearby town that Fat knew were there. They always got there early and
got the best spot. There weren't any good spots left and we only caught
one crappie in the whole stream. Anyhow, the high water had washed a
big dead hog into the midst of the brush there. Fat started teasing "Waldo"
(who had the "hot spot.") "How would you like a nice big slice or two of
that hog in a sandwich with mustard and Limburger cheese on rye?" Waldo
had a weak stomach and Fat knew it. Before long, Waldo said, "You damn
hog, Fat. I'll get you one of these days." He left, gagging. Of course we
nabbed the best spots before Waldo was out of sight.

We stayed at the camp, which was one room about 14'x16' with two
sides which we could swing out from about 4' high to about 8' and prop
it up with poles which made two sides and the front screen door. The
back had an old "chunk" stove. There was a 12' steel rowboat and later,
Fat made a 14' wooden rowboat. A half mile stretch up Pomeroy's dam
was flatter water, which was where the crappie hole was, and we used the
rest to "plug" for pickerel and some bass. We'd find the "pike," as we called
them, in weeds or near weeds, usually. The lure of choice was Johnson silver
minnow with pork rind attached. We liked it because it was very weedless
although expensive for us, but we seldom lost one unless the pike cut it off.
Bass fought better, but pike were vicious and got longer. We'd also hunt
squirrels out of the boat, because a corn field ran along the creek on one
side, so squirrels would be in the trees between the field and the creek.

One day we shot at a squirrel on a branch which hung over the water. It
wouldn't fall, but hid from us. We went upstream until we hit shallow water,
then came back to check the limb again. Just then the squirrel decided to
die, and nearly fell in the boat—close enough to splash water on me. I was
rowing at the time.

Fishing alone was not unusual for me even in those days, because of
construction jobs at Tuscarora Creek. I was at a favorite stretch with a
cliff on the opposite side, fishing an in-line spinner-fly combo, which was
a favorite then. In the smaller sizes, I caught trout, bluegills, rock bass,
smallmouth bass, fall fish, and the ever popular chubs. With split shot on,
I had been stuck on the bottom and gotten loose several times. I should
have changed or cut off some leader and retied it, but of course I wanted
to catch one more fish. Well, soon I had another strike on and it promptly
broke off my lure where the rigged mono was attached. Doggedly, I tied on

another spinner-fly and cast near the cliff again. Soon, I hooked another medium-sized fall fish—well, I didn't really hook the fish itself. I actually hooked the eye of the lure I had just lost with the fish still attached! What are the odds?! Not a big fish story, but a true one.

I did lose a really nice fish from the cliff side of that same pool one evening, on a helgramite. I never got to see it, but I figured it was a smallmouth bass.

Fishing the same spot a year earlier with my solid glass 8 ½' fly rod, it got hung up on the bottom. When jiggling the rod to loosen it, the tip came off the ferral and slipped all the way down to my hook. The rig finally broke, and the upper half of the Brute solid glass rod with it. Somehow it didn't bother me at all. No more achy wrists and cramped hands. It gave me an excuse to buy a decent fly rod, which I did the very next day. It's not good to be too frugal with fishing tools. You know, the important things.

Before Jess and I had our own cars, we would bum our parents' cars. Theirs was a 1937 Plymouth and ours was a 1938 Plymouth. Good cars for their time, but not Jeeps.

One evening after dark, I drove us back out a field, just weeds, no fences. We were tired but doing well until after we went through Port Royal, where while rounding a sharp turn, the lights went out. After a brief panic-stricken moment, I safely got the car stopped. Luckily, an old store at the Route 22 intersection was still open. We got some fuses and they worked—for about three miles. Another fuse installed and we got through Mifflintown. The last fuse fizzled in the (at that time) two-lane, but I was again able to get the car off the road safely. What to do? The only obviously logical thing was to wait for a slow moving truck. As the Plymouth was working well otherwise, we waited with the motor drumming until we saw a semi coming. NOW!!! We got back of it, but instead of the 40-45mph we expected, it was going about 65mph. Somehow I got that Plymouth up to speed and tailgated the semi, afraid to lose it in the darkness. Eventually, after a nerve-shattering trip, we made it to town and slowed to a normal speed. Guided by town traffic and street lights, we got home. God must look after the mentally ill and/or teenagers. Fortunately, there was an auto-electric shop near my parents' house and they fixed the short circuit the next day.

There was a gang of us at the cabin one spring day when the creek was in flood stage. We ran out of food, so the boys drove to the covered bridge below the dam. There were some ducks upstream in the flooded-over swamp where the water was calmer. They blasted one with 22's but couldn't get to it. The land owner, who thought he was a land baron, was at the nearest point of land, screaming at them, and guess who volunteered to retrieve the duck. "I'll get the boat and row over, and you guys have the truck (one of the guys' family flower truck) ready." I rowed to the point of land across from the cabin, and very nearly sunk the boat trying to get to the main current, as the boat hung up on a branch, forcing the upstream side under. Straining to the limit, I pulled the low side of the boat up while pulling on an upper branch with the other arm. Finally, I got into the wild main stream and rowed like mad for an opening in the trees near the crappie hole, which was now a raging torrent. I wasn't sure the boat would fit through, but I gave one last pump with the oars and then popped them into the boat. Scraping both sides, I made it through. The rest was easy. With the land baron screaming at us, I picked up the lead-infested duck and rowed up the exit to the covered bridge, to the van with its back doors open. The guys grabbed the boat as I got out and shoved it in the van. They said, "You must be crazy." Still shaking, I said, "Ah, nothing to it."

They actually did a good job of cleaning and cooking that duck, but I only ate a few bites because it tasted really strong. Probably all that lead.

Walking to the creek one day though waist high weeds, thinking about fishing, not worrying about snakes or anything, I suddenly realized I was about to step on a mama skunk and 3 or 4 little ones. Thanks to a teenager's reflexes, and fear of being sprayed, I somehow managed to do an about-face with only one foot on the ground—not unlike Wile E. Coyote going off a cliff and running back in mid-air. About 200 yards later, I thought, "Whew! She either didn't spray me, or missed." I later realized that even a skunk can't react that fast.

The summer previous to the "flood trip," Jess and I were fishing below the dam, and ran out of helgramites. Not up to gathering more, we were just goofing around on the way back to our mid-day meal of boiled hot dogs, baked beans out of a can, and 3-day-old coffee. (Jess' mom once claimed she couldn't sleep for three days after drinking our coffee.) Anyhow, crossing the stream by walking across the top of the dam, the water was very low. We noticed a big truck tire about mid-way across, with a huge snapping turtle stuck inside, obviously dead. Jess being more curious than I was, wondered why, hot as it was, there was no odor. Bad mistake! He just had to flip the tire upside down with the shell still stuck in it. All of the 20' or so was covered with maggots crawling. Jess said, "Funny—it still has no odor." Then a puff of air came toward us and we ran, gagging and puking, across the dam and up the shore as the stench hit us. Some things should not be tampered with. I like to think of these things not as stupid, but more as learning experiences. I also like to think that I wouldn't have flipped the tire if Jess hadn't done it.

After getting out of the Army a few years later. I wanted a solitary trip to Tuscarora Creek. For some reason, I tried an area I had never fished before. I lost myself in fishing and suddenly it was dark and I was a long way from the car. I decided to walk across the fields as there was very little moonlight. After crossing several fields, I didn't realize I was coming to the edge of one, and walked right into an electric fence that was waist high. It wouldn't have been so bad, but I was wearing a *big brass belt buckle* I had bought in Korea. It hooked on the wire and I couldn't get loose before I got ten or more hard jolts. I never wore that buckle again.

Jess and I were drafted about two weeks apart. I had to go first, and, feeling sorry for myself, decided to open trout season early, and did so in a remote area. Jess said, "You're nuts, you'll get caught." Two days later, he called and said, "Where are we going tomorrow? I just got my notice and have to go before trout season too." Well, we did go where we weren't likely to get caught. We had a good day, but didn't kill any fish—and didn't have a guilty conscience about it either, knowing there would be no fishing for at least two years. It would had to have been a cold-hearted warden that would fine us if we would have been caught.

We both got out of the Army two years later. Soon we were both married and fished together very little after that. Although we were always friends, we just drifted apart and did our own things. Jess got a job where he worked nights and specialized in fishing after dark, got a lot of big trout. I later got into fly fishing, but also did all types of other fishing.

CHAPTER THREE—THE RIVER

A lot of my younger years involved bass fishing the Juniata River, along with other native fish like fall fish, carp, rock bass, bluegills, crappies, and muskies. By the the spinning rods and reels were being improved more and more, along with monofilament line. When I went from my original Bach-Brown to a Luxor, it was a big jump in technology to me. I still have a Luxor reel. The pick-up spring was and still is a problem, which we learned to live with (and curse at.) However, we still used fly rods a lot, but with monofilament line as it worked better with bait. Flies were still in the future, except for some streamer flies and flies we put on in-line spinners.

Helgramites were the favorite, usually, in Tuscarora Creek as well as the river. The bigger, the better. Bass loved them as did pan fish and fall fish. A fellow I went to school with wanted to fish with our group, but didn't always fit in with our carefree, rotten attitudes, like when he wanted to know how to handle helgies without getting pinched. Well, I explained kindly, you pinch them by the tail and that paralyzes them. *Bad mistake!* The whole bait can went flying over the water with the day's worth of bait as the helgramite clamped on his pinkie and drew blood. I didn't know he knew all those nasty words.

Another time, there were two boats of us coming down the river after dark with two miles to the boat launch. It was dark as it could get with cloud cover as well. We had to go through a six foot wide opening in an old eel dam, and I was elected to guide us through the chute. Their reasoning was that since I had the worst eyes, I could see better in the dark. The motors were cut and we put the boats end-to-end. I stuck my head out the front of the lead boat, with several guys using oars to keep the boat aligned. "A little to the left, we're getting closer (and faster)—a little more—WHOA! *Right! Right!" Crash! Bam! Splash!* Well, no one was hurt, just the boats dinged up a bit. But my old school pal never went with us in a boat again. We made it back to the "take out" area without incident, as it was wider and deeper, and someone came with a flashlight. We had many after dark trips on the river, but no one else ever got upset over small mishaps. We kind of expected something every night we fished. Our wives never worried—unless they got a call from the police.

Another night I fished with my neighbor at that time, who was a good guy. We were fishing helgramites and wading and casting toward a pool by a limestone ledge. There was a bunch of Dobson flies (adult helgramites) that night. That didn't usually bother me. I had a big cigar that evening as all bugs were bothering us. Well, it was pitch dark out and we were catching some fish. Good, but just an average night. The cigar was down to a stub, then went out. I let out a string of bad words and Larry said, "What's wrong?" The Dobson flies were as thick as I've ever seen them. I said, "I didn't mind a few landing on my neck and arms, but when they land on my cigar butt just under my nose, that's enough! I quit for tonight." Larry readily agreed.

Upriver one drizzly day, in my home-made 10' boat, (a real death trap) I had a bunch of helgies and caught a few bass, but many more were swirling and dimpling the surface. I just couldn't fool them. Since I had some lures with me, I reluctantly put a small silver "flatfish" on a floater-diver. I fooled most all the bass I cast to after that. No huge ones—but nice nonetheless—and fun. That was my first successful experience of "thinking like a fish" and giving them what they wanted.

About that time I was working near the area that later became Three Mile Island. After work I'd go to a place where a stream came into the Susquehanna. There were limestone pools I could wade around and fish some bait I got from the stream. When I got downstream where the water was too large, I sometimes used my leftover bait and caught some pretty big catfish. I'd bring them back for the landlady where I roomed during the week, until she said, "No more catfish."

Often, I'd put a few lures in a small tackle box and fish them, as bait was hard to get in the stream near where I parked. Sometimes I'd get a few decent bass on a black "jitterbug" after dark on the way back. One night, a nasty thunderstorm was coming as I was about to quit. There was a nice pool about twenty by fifty feet where I was when it started to rain, and that was the wildest ten minutes of fishing for bass I've ever had. I hooked six fish and landed five (all between 15 and 18 inches) on five casts. One tossed the jitterbug soon after it was hooked and another grabbed it as soon as it hit the water. Then the storm really hit. Lightening and a deluge of rain poured as I ran up a thirty foot bank and across a two-lane road to my car. Before I could get my hip boots off, they were completely full of water; it rained that hard! Of course I was giggling the whole time. That's the kind of thing that keeps me coming back for more.

We often made drift trips down the Juniata from below Lewistown to Mifflintown. We would catch lots of smallmouth bass and other kinds of fish, no trophies, but lots of action. Occasionally, we'd get a walleye, but not often. They were usually in deeper water. This float usually had the boats scraping rocks, and more than once, the boats would have to be dragged over low places. Drinking water and coffee, and eating sandwiches gave us a nice noon break.

Wild Bill and I made a trip one day. Early on, it was very foggy over the water, and fishing was slow. "It'll get better as the sun burns it off," Bill said. "In the meantime, let's keep going to more productive water. "Sounds good," says me, as we had 10 to 11 miles total to float. Better to spend more time on good water. We drifted into an extra foggy area, looking to avoid rocks as we followed close to shore on the side where the flow was faster and a bit deeper. All of a sudden there was a big dead tree full of buzzards staring down at us. I don't know about Bill, but I had a chill start at my feet and not stop 'til it reached the top of my head. Spooky, but before long the mist burned off and the fishing picked up.

Bass fishing has been bad the last decade as a lot of bass died off with a virus or something. I hear it's a bit better now, and I hope the river gets back to the way it was.

Until muskies were introduced to the Juniata River, the biggest, most powerful fish was the carp. (Maybe they're still bigger, but I know they're powerful, although more predictable than the muskie.) Bill and I got on a "carp kick" one summer. We'd use crawdads, corn, and even strawberry and cherry dough balls made using Jello. We caught some, including after dark one time, one of the fellows with us was half asleep, and *zip!*—his rod flew into the river never to be seen again—at least by us.

One evening, I was fishing alone for bass, using soft-shelled crawdads. I had some left over, so after I went past the eel dam chute successfully, I anchored below an island and fished downstream after dark. There must have been a school of carp, hungry carp, and I had a ball with them until my bait gave out—even before my wrist did. I got six or eight, but no giants. I told my friend Bill about it and he was sorry he missed it. "Wild Bill," as many called him, wanted to try for carp with a fly rod soon, so we rigged some old fly rods with mono line and made some strawberry dough balls. Soon we were able to get together, went to a spot we thought would be good, and set up one fly rod each. I had hooked a couple, but they got off the hook both times. Bill got a small one, then soon after got a bigger one. The line hissed out almost all the way. Bill cranked it back in almost all the way, but the old "bugle mouth" ran the line out again, then again. Wild Bill was complaining how tired his wrist and forearm were getting when he got the big boy in close one more time. "Nice" me volunteered to be the net man, and just as Mr. Carp got close, I put the net in and splashed it around and panicked the carp and the line buzzed out again. Bill cursed me with traditional and newly invented words. Pretty loud too, but I was laughing so hard I didn't mind. He eventually insisted on netting the fish himself.

Whatever the rate of success we had, we always had fun. If we were trout fishing with flies, I could go where a trout rose and wait forever; it wouldn't rise again until Bill tried his luck. It was uncanny how often they would rise soon for Bill and he would get them.

Well, I eventually got some revenge. Muskie had been introduced several years before and were thriving in the Juniata. I wanted to go one morning and Bill couldn't go for a few hours, so I went alone. I was just tossing a big "Rebel" minnow from the shore at Jack's Creek where it flows into the Juniata. I had no strikes and was thinking of quitting, when on a cast I meant to stop my line and missed, the Rebel went into a big maple tree. Mumbling to myself, I ripped it out and it landed with a big splash with a bunch of leaves attached. I ripped it again, and the leaves came loose, and a three foot muskie smashed it instantly! I'll spare you the details of the battle, but since I had no net with me, I beached it on a muddy slope and picked it up by the eyes—a trick I learned in Canada with Northern Pike.

Walking back to the car, I saw Bill and his wife coming towards me. "Holy—! You lucky—!"
Wild Bill was never short of sweet talk.

CHAPTER FOUR—ICE FISHING

Hard water fishing is a sociable sport. Usually people like to fish near other people on the ice. People like to tell others their tales of the outdoors and just yak in general. It's not like on a trout stream where if you're a cast away, you're too close. The funny thing is that on the ice it doesn't seem to hurt the fishing, unless there's too much banging on the ice or the depth is too shallow and clear0.

When I first started, we used spuds. They're like a long handled chisel. I remember one winter going through 24' to 28' of ice. I really developed biceps that year.

The best improvements over the years were felt-lined boots, insulated coveralls, augers, (even power augers) tents, homemade huts, heaters, you name it. One year, a pair of fellows Wild Bill and I would see would have a barbeque grill on the ice and eat venison all day long. They had outdoor jobs and only occasionally worked in winter. They claimed they'd gain about 20 pounds each year, and lose it in the summer.

For a long while, we only used "tip-ups" with minnows. At first we had our homemade counter-balance ones, then different types of manufactured tip-ups, from the underwater kind, that triggered a spring to pop a flag up, then a magnetic type, then our favorite, the wind activated type that would jig our bait up and down. We were introduced to the little jigging rod with a very sensitive tip, for smaller pan fish, which I liked best of all for bluegills, perch, and crappies.

To set up, we drilled holes with augers, and to set the depth, we had weights with a spring clamp, and attached it to the hook and let it down 'til it hit the bottom. Then we'd bring it up according to how far we wanted it off the bottom, then fish it at that depth.

One time Bill and I showed an "educated" friend of ours how to set up, then went about doing ours. Our friend said, "Something's wrong with my tip-up. It keeps setting the flag loose." "Do you have a bite, maybe?" "No," he said, so Bill checked it and said, "You dumb—, it would help if you took the weight off after you get your depth!" (You just can't teach stupid.)

My one son and a friend of his came with Bill and me to Rose Valley Lake. The crappies there were nice, and on the feed. The boys, then about 13 years old, would get so excited they'd break the line when they'd set the hook. We were fast running out of jigs (small, tear-drop size) so we just put hooks on and stronger line. They had a blast!

Another old pal, Stan, built a special big red box with "Danger" painted on it, with a hole through it, and a homemade rig running through the hole. When the rig got a bite, a bell would be set off inside the box. We got it set up on a spot where bluegills were, and the bell was driving the other fishermen crazy. Sometimes I think Stan had too much time on his hands, but what a great friend. Stan would get cold, and on the way home he'd keep all his fishing clothes on and turn the heater on high. The rest of us would just about cook on the way home.

One day Stan got cold early and went to his van and had the heater going, and this fellow in a white fur-lined parka knocked on his window and said, "Catching any, fellow?" Apparently, the man was gay. Stan rolled the window up and drove away. Stan wasn't afraid of much, but that scared him.

Another group, another lake, and it was cold. Some fish were being caught, and talking to some other people, one guy was bragging about his teaberry wine (laced with brandy) he made. We talked him into going to his vehicle to get some for us to taste. Well, about half an hour later he returned. The bottle was down to about two inches and he was a bit snookered. We did each get a small taste and it was *great!*
I hope the wine maker got home safe.

The first Martin Luther King Day, I had off, as I worked a federal job, U.S Post Office. The ice was new and safe, and I headed to Blanchard Dam at Howard. I just had waxworms and two jigging rods, and headed for the far side away from most of the fishermen. I set up my rods and lawn chair and started to pour coffee from my thermos, when I picked up a rod and caught a nice big crappie. Then my other rod bounced and I picked up another slab. Not huge, but nice fillet size. I got so busy my coffee got cold, and the action didn't stop! What a fun day! I called other guys over, kept 22, returned many, and we all got a bunch. Everyone deserves a day like that. I must have drilled my hole over a huge school in about 20 feet of water. Often, the jig sweetened with waxworms never got down all the way, and the line would veer off with another fish. About four o'clock I ran out of waxworms and quit. Some people called me over and offered me more bait, but I didn't want to be a hog. I was already blessed with a great day and great weather.

One afternoon I went to Faylor Dam near Beaver Springs. It's a shallow Game Commission lake with lots of bluegills, usually on the small side. There were just a few people on the ice and late in the day sometimes the bluegills turn on. I just wanted enough for one good meal for my wife and me. After ten keepers, I decided to leave as it was getting dark soon and I didn't bring a light. I noticed one other person fishing not too far out, and he was catching some. He was sitting on a boat cushion directly on the ice. I went toward him as I headed back to my truck and asked, "How you making out?" "Not bad, for a late start," says he. Then I noticed he had an artificial leg. "You're a tough S.O.B., coming out here alone. Can you move on the ice OK?" "Yeah, I don't have any problem—I'm not going to let that bother my life style." I said, "That's a great attitude." "It's too bad more people don't feel that way." I went on to tell him about a fellow I worked with at Aberdeen Proving Ground. He was at Edgewood Arsenal, and a bomb that they were moving went off, and he lost his one leg, arm, eye, and got a lot of shrapnel. "Oh, by the way, look at this"—and pulled his other pant leg up, and he had another artificial leg. I said, "You're an inspiration." He replied, "When I first had this happen, I thought, either get up off my ass and live, or sit in a room and stare at the wall. I made the right decision."

CHAPTER FIVE—POSTAL STORIES

I was a letter carrier for twenty six years. I hesitated to mix this in with the fishing and outdoor tales, but I guess these true stories might help explain about the way I think. Plus, they helped my attitude when I had bad days. The thing that irked me mainly was "too many chiefs, not enough Indians."

For the most part I had great coworkers. One girl that worked as a clerk was most always in a good mood—joking, etc., and also a good worker. The only time she was in a bad mood was when Penn State football lost a game. (Which in those days, was not too often.) Anyhow, one day it was a scorcher when I came in off the route. At a sink in our work area, I threw some cold water on my sweaty face and partly thin hair, and pulled a comb out to put what hair I had in place. She walked by giggling and said, "I don't know why you even carry a comb." In one of my fastest and cruelest comebacks ever, I said, "You wear a bra, don't you?" It was the first time I ever saw her speechless. One of the nearby female R.D. carriers tried to stifle a laugh, but couldn't.

There was a local pioneer airplane pilot who was legendary for some of his exploits. Supposedly he flew under one of our local river bridges one time. Anyhow, he had recently passed away, and his ashes came through the mail, as was often the case in those days. One carrier was extremely goosey about getting near any of those parcels. I had to go down to the restroom, and on the way back I went into the "junk room" and found a box about the same size as the pilot's remains. I filled the box with scrap paper and ran some tape around it. Going back up, I yelled out to the goosey carrier. As he turned around, I tossed the paper-filled box to him and said, "Jacques' last flight!" I thought sure he'd have a heart attack as he tried to dodge it while squeaking out a "Noooo, NO! Oh No!"

We had a rural carrier, Paul, who was a hard worker, conscientious, quiet, and a good family man. There were times when he had to stop at a small post office in a neighboring town to pick up more mail to deliver in addition to his regular route. The pipsqueak, self-important Post master there tried to lord it over Paul and harass him as much as possible. Paul was becoming a nervous wreck trying not to rebel or worse, "pop" this idiot Post Master and get fired or punished by some higher authority. Word got back to our office, and one Saturday one of our clerks decided to do something about it. There were no supervisors on Saturdays (they *never* worked on Saturdays—even though, on my last day before retirement, I was given *mandatory* overtime on a Saturday.) Anyhow, this clerk was smooth talking, and somewhat of a loose cannon. He decided to call this egotistic Post Master and straighten him out.

"This is Inspector Kumpfmaier from your regional office in Harrisburg, and I want to speak to Post Master (so&so.)"

"This is him, Sir!"

Anyhow, this clerk had the Post Master "sir"-ing him for a full fifteen minutes, giving him *hell* about treating good employees like dirt, and if he didn't start treating this rural carrier and the rest of his workers better, he would find someone else to do his job.

When the telephone was hung up, everyone in our office applauded. The lord of the small post office never suspected anything, and later was reported to have asked our P.M., "Who is this Kumpfmaier from regional?" Our P.M. said he didn't know all the big shots. He also didn't know about the call. Our rural carrier never had any more problems at that small office. By the way, that clerk, "Don," was also the best poker player I ever met.

There were other hijinks in our office, like the time two carriers were horsing around when the mail was light, and one pushed the other around in a large hamper and almost ran into the Post Master.

"You men better grow up and do your jobs. If you don't have enough to do, I'll find work for you." They didn't know the P.M. was there that day.

There were dog problems from time to time. One year I was bitten six times, not badly, but once it could have been nasty. I had certified mail to get signed about eighty feet from my truck, and two large, mean German shepherds came charging after me. I was young and in good shape then, and I took off for the postal van and jumped in and slid the door shut just as the dogs arrived. The man came up the walk and apologized, and said, "That's the worst thing you could have done by running."

"Well," I said, "I knew I could make it to the truck in time, but I didn't know what the dogs would do if I had stayed there."

Part of my route was walking, and some was delivering rural style. (The Post Office vehicles had the driver's side on the right, so you could stick mail in a mailbox without getting out.) One time I was at the turn-around point. There had been snow, so I had chains on, and one of them broke and was slapping the truck loudly, like I was inside a steel drum and someone was beating on it like mad. I was partly under the truck wiring the chains back together, when I saw eight legs of two *huge* dogs. I thought, Oh shoot! Well, I had to get out sometime, so I stuck my head out and got licked sloppy. The owner was there and apologized, and I said, "No problem, they're nice dogs. Man, but they're big though—what do you feed them?" Max, the owner of the farm, said, "Once the grass starts growing, I don't feed them anything—they live off groundhogs!"

I also had some crazies on my route. One was very wild-eyed and lived with a woman I named (to myself only) Little Annie Rooney eyes. She always had a big grin but never seemed to focus on anything. One time the temporary boyfriend said to me, "If you don't bring my check tomorrow, I'll kill you." I reported him to the Post Master, and they shortly took him away, so I never had to deal with him again.

When I was a sub, there was another mean dog named Ginger. A state trooper owned him. When I walked that route, Ginger would walk the two blocks up and back with me, and threaten any other dog that came near me. For some reason, Ginger loved me.

Welfare people were a way of life for a mailman. There were three kinds. Most were people that really needed the money and probably should have got more benefits. Some should have been in institutions of some type; they had no idea how to budget money. Then there were what we called "porch monkeys." Some had been on welfare for three generations or more. One would follow me on check day with his beat-up station wagon until I stopped once and walked back and asked why he was in back of me. He just wanted his check. I said, "You go wait at your mail box till I get there. I get really nervous when I have all these checks, and already notified the police and Post Master. I don't know who might be following me with intent to rob." He stopped following me.

Another "wacko," Ben, had his mailbox attached to a post and stuck in concrete blocks. He made his own newsletter in which he bad-mouthed city officials and any other kind of authority. He wandered around with a briefcase with his newsletter and a bottle of wine in it. His unfinished house was disintegrating and was no longer fit to live in, so he lived in his garage. At one time Ben was a school teacher, but somewhere along the line some of his wires crossed and he was never the same again. Ben started to mess with me when I first started, but I wouldn't take it. He would move his mailbox from place to place, higher and lower. One time I caught him giggling and got out of my truck. I went to him and pointed right in his face. "Ben, you're not fooling with city hall or the mayor or the Post Office now. You're messing with me and making my job harder. I'm not going to report you to anyone, but if you keep this up I'm going to kick your butt up one side and down the other." No more problems.

One other porch monkey would waddle like a duck all over the area on nice weather days, usually with her daughter that walked the same way. Later, her daughter had kids, also fatherless.

I delivered to the local UniMart one nice sunny day and she was there. (The clerk told me she had to watch her close, for stealing.) Anyhow, she looked at me and said, "I'd love to have your job. I like to walk." I said, "Hon, I just wish you had any job." She didn't even get insulted.

Before I had my own route, I delivered wherever they needed me. There was one of the few old family neighborhood stores left this day, and the old guy that ran it loved to tell jokes. I told him one about this new welfare doll that was out. It had this big key on its back that you wound up all the way and it didn't do a damn thing. The old guy loved it and would tell all the porch monkeys when they came in, not caring if they got mad.

The bad part about my job was that I never had a Saturday break day because of our six day work week. The good part was that I had days off in the middle of the week and often had the fishing all to myself.

CHAPTER SIX—THE PATH TO BROADWATER

Before I became a regular carrier, when I was a P.T.F. (part time flexible) at the post office, I never had a regular schedule. Sometimes when I got a Wednesday break day, I'd get together with Pete, my barber, and Dick, my insurance agent. On Tuesday after work, we'd fish several hours, stay overnight at Dick's camp near Poe Valley, and fish the next day.

This one Tuesday was beautiful weather, and we elected to fish Penn's at Poe Paddy Park. As it was early May and we didn't fish flies much then, we decided to "egg" them (use salmon eggs.) We had fun and killed three fish, releasing some also. I lucked into a 20" brownie that Dick had swiped at several times, then netted after I threatened him, For some reason, we decided to quit early and go to camp for supper. We plopped the three trout onto a newspaper on the back seat floor of Dick's International Scout, and proceeded through the campground, which oddly enough was empty except for one person at one of the old lean-tos. The camper waved us over to find out how we did, and we showed him the fish on the back seat floor.

"Wow, they're really nice, especially that one. What did you get 'em on?"

Never one for a straight answer, I said, "Did you ever see those mini colored marshmallows? I got a pack of them and that's what I got the big one on."

He appeared satisfied and we went on our way and forgot all about it. We fished the next day on Poe's, as it had rained in the night and got Penn's muddy.

That Friday after work, I stopped at Pete's shop to get my hair cut. As soon as Pete saw me, he started laughing so hard he had to stop cutting his customer's hair.

"What's so funny, Pete?" I inquired.

"You wouldn't believe it," he answered. "The first person that came in the shop Thursday morning, before six o'clock AM, said, 'Guess what they're catching them on at Penn's Creek?! Marshmallows!'"

And you think women spread rumors fast!

To this day, forty years later, we still chuckle about that episode.

My first memory of fishing downstream from Poe Paddy Park on Penn's Creek is my first memory of catching a nice brown trout on a dry fly. (An "Adams" tied by a hunchback man almost ninety years old. Much later, I met his son, now ninety years. Good genes in that family.) It was a hot summer day, and Tom, a bass fishing friend, wanted to show me more of Penn's besides the area near the road. Even at that age, I was struck by the beauty and wildness of the area. We knew little of fly fishing then, so we used Adams flies because he said, "It's the only fly you'll ever need, because it represents lots of different bugs." It's still probably one of the best all-purpose flies. I was casting away and I must have done everything right at this one pretty pocket near the far shore. With the high sun and the clear water, I watched the Adams fly drift into the small pool, and very casually a nice 12" or 13" brown slowly rose and calmly ate my fly. I don't remember any wild or vicious fight, but I'll always remember how confidently that trout took my fly.

Usually at that time, we fished with a gang. It took a long time for me to realize how spooky trout can be, even in bigger streams. This one time we were walking out as it was getting dark and an owl started to swoop at us. One of the guys, Jack, was terrified of it. We must have been in its territory because it tried to scare us every time we walked that part of the path. Jack seldom went in that direction after that, and never after dark. It never bothered the rest of us, or at least we never let on we were spooked by it.

Broadwater was our name for a pool about a quarter mile in length that had a "break" or bit of current halfway through it. The path on the other side was an old railroad bed that was originally used mainly for logging purposes. At Poe Mills, the village that used to house loggers and such, the railroad went across a trestle, through a tunnel, and went parallel to Penn's Creek toward the village of Weikert, four or five miles downstream. We'd often go down that side to fish different water. At that time it was designated fly fishing only after you got through the tunnel. One time, our group split up, and Stan was going to scare Don when he came back through the tunnel. When we were through for the evening, it got dark as the devil's heart. Stan got positioned in back of a ledge. Naturally we had no flashlights with us. Soon he heard boots picking the way through the pitch black tunnel, and Stan waited until Don was just past him. Stan let out this loud squawk of the great horned owl. The footfalls became an all out sprint. Stan chuckled all the way back to the car, where Don was in his street clothes smoking a cigarette. Stan, still giggling, said, "I guess I got you back in the tunnel just now." Don said, "Got me what? I've been back for half an hour." We all laughed and wondered who he scared the crap out of.

One year we'd often see an albino deer about half way. It appeared to be pure albino and we never heard of anyone shooting it in deer season. We never saw it after that summer, but a partial, or piebald one was in the area the next year. My friend Stan had a chance at it in bow season, but declined to shoot. "It was just a cute little bugger," he said. "I just didn't have the heart." He killed other deer other years, so it must have been the size or the odd color. I had a part albino near camp years later, that I often saw, six miles or more over the mountain.

Going alone one spring morning, I heard pattering in the leaves and looked around, and here came a gray squirrel charging toward me—followed by about ten or twelve more. What the heck!! They chased the first gray up one tree and down another all around me, and weren't bothered by my presence at all. They came within a few feet of me. This went on for a good ten minutes and I was amazed at their endurance and persistence. Finally, they were out of my sight. Was the first squirrel in heat, or did it rob a squirrel bank? Burn the squirrel flag? I told other people about this, including a game warden, but never got a clear answer—just theories.

There are lots of porcupines in this area too. Different times, I returned to my vehicle at dusk and saw them not much higher than my head in a tree, or on the ground. I think I was more worried about walking into them after dark than I was of stepping on a rattlesnake. A son of the camp owner where I parked, owned a really nice, but dumb, dog. One day, returning to my truck for a lunch break, Bob asked me to help him with pulling porky quills out of the dog. We got most of them out and the poor dog was hurting for a while. That evening, I was headed downstream and by-passed some people who were fishing by walking through the woods. Soon I saw a porky nearby. Spotting Bob downstream, I veered over and told him he'd better keep the dog near him, as the dog was roaming all over. Sure enough, the dog got in the porky again, and this time Bob had to take him to the vet. I believe that same dog got quilled at least two more times.

One time I was at the lower end of Broadwater, just where I'd cross to fish down through the islands. I was scanning the flat water for fish feeding on top, when I heard something beside the big tree on my right. I slowly peeked around and there was a mink preening itself on a flat rock. I slowly brought my fly rod around and tapped him on the head. He turned to see what it was, then when he saw me, quickly did the Houdini act.

One of the cutest catches I ever made was ten feet up from that same spot. Nothing much doing that day, I was just looking for rising fish. The water was low and clear. It was hot out and I was sitting on the three foot bank with my legs dangling down. I thought I kept hearing a fish slurping, but couldn't locate it. A slight current swung toward me and the bank, and flowed back under the bank. I heard another slurp and noticed a small wake coming from under the bank—too close to cast, and if I tried to move I'd spook the fish. I gave it a long think, then tied a floating ant on and flipped it carefully above the rock that caused the flow to go under the bank. I managed to get some slack in the line so it would go with the flow. Probably catch a root! The ant disappeared and two seconds later I heard "slurp!" and tightened. The circus was on. Once the fish headed for open water I was OK. It turned out to be 14-15" which surprised me. For once, I didn't get in a hurry and did the correct things.

Just downstream on the second island, I had some other odd happenings. I was crossing over one fine spring day to approach a nice spot, when I caught movement near my left, upstream side. It was a groundhog and he started to walk out an almost horizontal maple tree that was leaning over the water. The chuck walked toward the narrow end and I almost expected him to fall into the water. All he wanted was to get at the tasty fresh leaves at the tip of the tree. He was still eating when I started to go downstream.

A big snake was in front of me and I let him go under a bush. Let sleeping snakes alone, I always say. Then I saw another snake under another bush. Before I got in the water I saw five or six snakes on that little island. Was it a snake breeding place or what? I don't even know what kind they were because I didn't care to get that close or to bother them. If I had to guess I'd say they were water snakes. Of the many times I've been on that island before or since, I never saw another snake there.

However, another day, my nephew Bill that I introduced to fly fishing, was fishing on the other side nearby, into a brush pile about a rod's length away, and a big (according to Bill) rattlesnake was ready to jump over and bite him. Did you ever hear of a rattler make a 10' or 12' jump to attack someone that was in the water? He said it just startled him, but he would never fish that area again.

On the subject of Bill and rattlesnakes, he had been on Broadwater until dark one night when the green drakes were emerging. The stream gets crowded then like it's the first day on a stocked area. Anyhow, he came chuckling into the parking lot where the rest of us were telling stories about the evening's fishing. He told about this "hog" that was trying to catch everything in a 360 degree range from where he was stationed in the middle of Penn's in the best part. The guy was up to his belly button; it was quite dark, and on shore, Bill was taking his rod apart. He heard this loud scream: "Holy Mother of God!" then wild splashing as the hog tried to walk on water to get out of the stream. He claimed a big rattlesnake had tried to swim out on him.

Some of the annoying things were "fire rings" where people (canoers) would camp illegally. We would destroy these regularly. Some would soon be rebuilt, which we also destroyed. The ones which irked us the most were the out-of-state fish wardens that camped yearly along the edge of the shore, with the permission of the fish commission. They had a huge fire ring, wrote names, dates on the stones with charcoal and crayons. Nice example for the rest of us. The high officers and director _will_ hear about this. The offenders were from Ohio or Indiana, I believe. If they want to give them a courtesy, let them float 2-3 miles and give them keys to the fish commission building and let them hog up *their* property.

I have, at my risk, told people not to camp, put out fires, no motorized vehicles, etc. So have some of my fellow fishermen.

I think my friend Walt might have cured a motorcyclist from driving two miles to the midsection of the artificial lures area. After us two old farts struggled in hot weather, with waders and all our gear on, we saw this bike parked along the railroad bed. Ol' Walt looked up and down the walkway, and, seeing no one, he got out his pocket knife and cut the fuel line. Then he plugged each end with a piece of wood and put the line back together with matching black tape. "We won't be the only tired puppies tonight—or whenever that lazy biker gets home," Walt quipped as we both grinned and went fishing. I imagine that bike got pretty heavy after pushing it a mile or two on the cinder bed. (Unless he had a flashlight, and figured out the trouble, which I doubt.)

Tubers (that is, people floating downstream on innertubes) were also disturbing, but didn't bother me too much as long as they didn't litter or linger. One day, I was fishing in front of Swift Run, beside an island, when I heard 15 or 20 coming down. I sighed and moved back out of the way. This adult woman and her daughter actually rammed me, and I mentioned that they forgot to get their drivers' licenses for the tubes. "Mom" snottily said I should have moved out of their way (I was almost on shore.) So, patiently, I thought I'd hike a half mile downstream where they always took their tubes out, then hike back through the tunnel on a nice path, back to where the tubers started. I was fishing just past where their the take-out place was, and here comes Mom and her daughter, leaders of the pack. I hesitantly told them they passed the take-out place.

"I know where I am! Don't you get smart with me!"

"Sorry," I grinned, "I didn't mean to offend you."

Soon, they were several hundred yards down Penn's Creek, past some fast riffles, and the rest of the pack was getting out at the correct place. Madonna and child were looking at a bank which was almost like a cliff, with loose cinders, and it was tough rough walking to go back along the shore. So, they in their flip-flops, struggling back up the cliff, clawing and grabbing, and scratching their dainty knees, hands and feet, to the railroad bed about 125 feet straight up. Of course, I could have suggested to them that they cross to my side and walk up a nice, smooth path, then cross the stream to the correct spot, but I didn't want to get bad-mouthed again.

Occasionally, things don't go as planned. One evening, I was in a hurry to get to Broadwater to catch a spinner fall. I'd pack a rucksack from time to time with my waders, vest, wading shoes, drinking water, and sometimes a lunch. It saved walking a mile in hot weather in waders, and even with the pack, it was easier and cooler. This evening, I arrived ready to fish, except for one thing: my rod. After I pounded my fist on a tree for awhile, I returned for my rod. I didn't mind the extra walk as much as the time missed fishing. I wasn't the only one, either. Wild Bill forgot his reel one evening. I went back with him, in case it fell out of his vest on the way. Fortunately, he found it in his vehicle.

It gets very cool in the spring evenings, even when the day may have been quite warm. An old school chum was in the area one day and just wore a T shirt and was freezing early. I loaned him a warm shirt. He was book-smart, a good fly-tier, but had no common sense. The red quill spinner fall was on, and I slipped in over my wader top right by the shore. I took my shirt back so I could catch a few more fish without freezing. Carl was angry with me, but I said I'd rather be a cad than cold.

THE MOVIE

I ran into Bernie one day in the parking lot at Broadwater, and after telling each other how we were doing lately, he asked, "How would you like to make a movie on Penn's Creek?"

After realizing that he was serious, and that a friend of his he had met in the Bahamas was a camera man in the film industry, I agreed to try, just for a lark. Bernie asked if I knew any other retired Penn's Creek fanatic. I soon thought of Bobby, another camp owner by the old railroad bed. Knowing him, Bernie readily agreed. After talking to Bob, he agreed to give it a try.

Bernie introduced me to the camera man, John Pitka, from the Slippery Rock area. John's brother was pretty successful in the business, and John and Bernie wanted to do this as a fun thing, with a possibility of making a series of different types of shows. They later did one on women's fishing, and one on steelhead, but they weren't too successful.

Anyhow, John came to my truck to meet me, and like a fool, I said, "Why don't you get a haircut and take those girly earrings off?" Luckily,

John—about 6'3" and husky and rough looking—didn't kill me. I guess he thought anyone small as I am that would say that to him might pull a gun on him. Anyhow, we got along good, and he lugged that huge camera, plus a big bag of extras around the steep, rocky, bushy country and wouldn't accept any help. They didn't want a lot of fish-catching shots like in the bass shows you see on TV. We did a good discussion on green drakes on Bobby's camp front porch, some nice scenery, and more talking while we each cast for the camera. I still had a big green drake fly on from the week before, but didn't embarrass myself when casting. The other two did much better than I did when talking, but I was able to catch a brown on cue for the camera next day, when fishing nymphs. That was the hardest thing to do—between hatches, some flies, but a few rises, people all over the stream, and clear water with the sun out bright. That's why I decided to use nymphs, as I figured a better chance to catch a fish that way for the film. I actually got three OK browns, but they only put one in the film. This 20 minute show was actually on PBS several times, and that was my five minutes of fame.

They were never able to work a deal to make more shows, and Hollywood never called me to be on the "big screen," which is all right. I'd rather go fishing on my own. Besides, I wouldn't know what to do with all the money and fame.

I've been known to carry a book with me often when I expected the fishing to be slow. I don't feel like nymphing sometimes, and would rather fish dry flies, so when the rises were few, I'd often find a likely spot and pull out a paperback and a cigar (at that time of my life,) and plop streamside and read and listen.

One blustery morning it was spitting some rain, and the March browns were active, but not thick. I had fooled some, but it was slow, so I got a book out and read and listened. When a trout takes a big size 10 March brown as it skitters across flat water, it usually makes a slurp or splash. Every time I heard a "take" I'd try to locate it and get a good drift over it with my artificial.

There was another angler that came down to fish across the creek from me, and wasn't doing too well. What he didn't realize was that the wind was blowing across the stream and down toward me. March browns will stay on the water quite a while in that type of weather, fluttering and trying to get dry so they can fly into the trees.

Every so often, while reading, I'd locate a fish, and if the wind would let me get an accurate cast, the trout would take it immediately. This happened with three or four fish. As soon as I landed and released the brown, I'd go back to reading until I located another. This drove the other fisherman nuts, and soon he was on my side of Penn's, wanting to know how I could just cast once every five or ten minutes and catch a fish, then calmly sit down and read again. Rather than let him think I was a great fisherman, I explained how the wind was blowing toward me and bringing the big flies along, also how there was no use casting unless I located a feeding fish. I could see the reasoning settle in his face as he said, "Well, hell, I should have noticed that!" Then he caught some too, and moved downstream so I could have my spot. Another riddle solved—temporarily.

That's the kind of thing that makes people addicted to fly fishing. It doesn't happen every trip out. Often there's nothing to figure out. Sometimes the trout are not feeding on top, because there's nothing on top to eat. Other times there's a great emergence of flies, and all one has to do is match the artificial with the natural and drift it naturally to where the trout is feeding. It's a great game, and the more you learn about the different bugs' habits and the trouts' preferences, the more fish you'll catch. Sometimes!

Another day, the blue-winged olive duns were emerging sporadically all day long. I had that day off and I was on the stream early, for me, and covered a lot of stream. There were just enough flies emerging and just enough fish rising to keep me going. It was almost 6PM, so I went back upstream to a favorite spot, still a ways downstream from Broadwater and about a mile from the car. This was a good time to take a break, so I took my vest off and got out my lunch, water, and book. I was about finished eating when my friend Jim appeared. He said, "How on earth can you sit there reading when there are trout rising all around?"

"I don't have to catch every trout in the stream," says me. "I'll get back to them soon. I need to change flies anyhow, as this one is all beat up from fish." Actually, I wanted to change to a spentwing pattern, as it was that time of day. That worked even better, as now the fish were eating the more plentiful spentwings, as the flies came back to the creek to lay their eggs.

This was one of those days when everything went according to plans. It doesn't always, in fact, seldom works like that. I got back to the car before dark, as I had a good day, and the trout were still rising when I quit.

One more story where I get to toot my own horn a bit: I was beginning to fish Penn's Creek one day as a couple of neighborhood kids playing hooky were starting. They were new at fly fishing, and saw me catch several trout, and wanted to know what to use. I gave them some caddis flies and put them on some rising trout. The older one, Mickey, was a nice kid, but really loud and boisterous. Soon he thought he was the world's best and was teasing me: "I got five and you only got two."

"Mickey," I said, "I can catch any fish. I've just been putting you on the easy ones." (Me and my big mouth.)

"Well," Mickey said, "if you're so good, catch that one."

"Where?" I said. "I don't see any."

"Over there, behind that lone rock, on the opposite shore."

Then I saw the rise. It was a foot down current on the wrong side of a three foot long narrow rock.

"No problem," I said. (Again, me and my big mouth.)

I started a long cast and thought I'd better get it right the first cast, or it would drag and spook the trout. That would really set Mick off with another barrage of bad-mouthing me. I'm not the world's best caster, but I do fair. After a short "think," I made a side-arm cast and stopped the line early, and in mid-air, it hooked in a right angle and the fly drifted perfectly down to the 11" trout. He inhaled it. There wouldn't have been a second chance. After landing and releasing the trout, I asked Mick if he had any other easy ones for me to catch. That set Mickey off: "That's the luckiest thing I ever saw!"

"I'm going downstream a ways," I said. "You boys have fun." I got out of there fast before any more challenges could be made. I enjoyed a big grin from Kevin, the younger hooky player. I think he enjoyed the coup as much as I did.

The bad part was that I never saw Mickey on a trout stream again. I hope that episode didn't discourage him, because he would have made a good angler if he'd leave his adding machine at home. Kevin still fishes and is active in Trout Unlimited.

We had names for most of the spots on the stream: "the Cable Hole," "the Triangle Rock," "the Spot below the Cable," "the Spring Hole," "the Willow Hole," "the Islands," "the Clay Bank Hole," (why are fishing holes called "holes"?) "Aumiller's Flats," and "Rainbow Riffle." (There have been no rainbow trout, except "accidentals," for years in Penn's.) and many other hot spots.

Early, probably in the 1960's, several of our group, and several of another gang, were all trying unsuccessfully at a nice brown sucking March brown flies tight to the rock at Triangle Rock. No one could reach it without the fly dragging, and the water was high and no one was willing to wade closer. Except me, of course. To get a natural drift, one had to cast upstream, so I waded downstream just about as far out as I dared, near the top of my chest waders. I had my "sissy stick," as most sensible anglers use a wading staff. On my tip-toes in fast water, I stripped line out as far as I could cast, and while the wind was still, I let it fly and barely got past the rock. Sure enough, the big brown came up and inhaled the fly. Well, being on my tip-toes in swift, cold water to the top of my waders, plus my excitement, I naturally struck too hard and broke him off. As I got back to the safety of the shallower, slower water, one of the other gang was cursing me for blundering the strike: You dumb, clumsy, son of a blankety-blank, so-and-so!

Even though he was bigger than me, I gave it right back to him.

"At least I got him to eat my fly, that's more than anyone else could do." (And got back to shore without drowning, I thought to myself.)

It was a rainy day one June and I was off work, so naturally I went to Penn's Creek and took my rod for a walk. By-passing some nymphing-type water, hoping to find some surface action, I eventually made my way past Broadwater. With still no surface action, I decided to nymph. There was always food for trout under the water. Besides, with the rain really pelting down hard now, the trout probably couldn't see any bugs on top anyhow. Rigging with a large stone nymph, I decided to fish through the islands, which basically are several smaller streams. I hadn't nymphed this stretch for a while, and with the rain pounding hard, it helped mask my form from the trout.

I caught several decent browns shortly, then, due to a worn leader, lost a dandy when it broke off. So, I waded under a small tree to re-rig. While doing so, I was startled to see three people by-passing me. I thought, "What the hell are they fishing in this hard downpour for?" Knowing the folks, I realized we all had good rain gear on, and we could have all stayed home to clean the attic or garage. After thinking about it, I knew we weren't so dumb after all.

I switched to fishing left-handed for a while and actually caught several, but although I could cast left-handed, OK but not great, I had trouble using my right hand for line control. I quit soon regardless, because my right hand was sore and tender from a recent carpal tunnel procedure.

I chuckled to myself on the way back up, thinking of another hard downpour one time when Wild Bill and I were in my little pram casting and trolling wet flies. A horn tooted at us, and we later found out it was our friend Stan and his wife. She asked, "Who would be crazy enough to be out fishing in a small boat on a day like this?"

Stan answered, "The only ones I can think of are Denny and Wild Bill." He found out later he was right.

Tom wanted me to prove to him about the blue wing olive spinner fall, during nice weather and civilized evening fishing, so soon we headed for Penn's, and because there were anglers on the nearby water, we went downstream to the pocket water above Broadwater. There were usually nicer fish there, but tougher to fool. Sure enough, the fish started feeding and we each got a couple. Then they fed harder and faster. We located some nice browns, but proceeded to get humbled as only a trout with a pea sized brain could humble even pretty good fly rodders like us.

Naturally, we were the last ones to get to the parking lot. It was already near dark as we loaded up my pick-up, and got our waders off. Guess what? Flat tire. Like the proverbial pancake. Neither of us having an engineering degree, we couldn't figure out how to get the spare tire loose from beneath the vehicle. The hinged crank-up thing was supposed to fit into a notch and turn just so, then the tire should come loose. After an hour lying on the rocky ground in the now pitch dark with a flashlight, we gave up.

Grabbing our total of five flashlights, we started the six mile hike over the mountain to where Tom's pick-up was at my camp. I didn't trust his truck because it hadn't been working well. The two or three mile hike up the one side of the mountain wore out two of the flashlights and my legs. I don't do well going up hills. Coming down the other side, I got my second wind (or legs) and Tom began to suffer from his new sneakers rubbing. The batteries in the other flashlights were about done, and it was darker than a witch's heart. We finally reached a clearing at a camp in Havice Valley. We both came to a dead stop when we saw the sky after coming out of the tree canopy. The stars were twinkling brighter than I have ever seen them. After looking at each other kind of startled, I said to Tom, "I thought we were in Roswell, New Mexico there for a while.

Despite the flashlights being about done, we could now see well enough to reach camp. Tom's truck sputtered and skipped, but it managed to get us home.

"Except for a few minor problems, it was a very interesting evening," Tom quipped as we parted.

CHAPTER SEVEN—OUT WEST

Starting in the 1960's, some of our trout fishing gang would go to Montana when we could get enough money, people, and time off. Ideally, it would be four people in a pick-up with two bunks in the back. This way, two would be up front, driver, and "shot-gun" to make sure the driver had directions and that he didn't fall asleep. A trip was usually two weeks, and we'd pitch a tent and do our own cooking at each stop. This way it was much cheaper, plus we could camp closer to where we fished. The cost per angler at first was two hundred to two fifty for two weeks.

On my first trip, there were three of us, and we pulled a twenty two foot trailer. Although comfy, the cost ran about three hundred fifty each, with much more gasoline for the powerful truck, and higher campground fees. We weren't sure we'd have enough money to get home. I do remember the morning in Yellowstone Park as we were preparing to leave. It was about 17degrees F out (we had a gas heater.) Dave said to get rid of the rest of the coffee. It turned out three "hippies" were camped in a pup tent next door. Two girls and a boy. We gave them the coffee in Styrofoam cups. They were about frozen and thought we were gods.

Later that trip, we had been in the "boonies" for about a week, and decided to treat ourselves to a restaurant meal. It was delicious and I was a bit giddy, and started to giggle to myself. Dave, always the cool one, asked "What's so funny?"

I whispered, "Look at those guys at the table across the room talking with their mouths full."

It turned out they were deaf-mutes and they were talking sign language. Dave was embarrassed at my bad sense of humor, but no one else noticed except us. I just can't help myself sometimes. I did notice Paul grin about it.

Out of six trips to Montana, my memories get tangled, and I've heard of the other's trip so often, I feel like I also was on some of their trips.

On another trip with Dave, we fished the Boulder downstream to the Yellowstone River. Dave did like adventure. Once, he took pictures of a big bull elk, lying down, from about twelve feet away. I was afraid the elk wouldn't like it, but as Dave stayed down and moved slowly, it didn't get upset. Of course, I was about fifty feet away. Anyhow, fishing the Boulder sown to Yellowstone, we were naturally caught in the dark with no flashlights. There was a herd of semi-wild cattle on the way back, and I was terrified, rightfully so, that they would charge. They did! They made six or eight false charges, and we yelled and screamed at them and threw stones. One came within five feet of me and I clonked him with a softball-size stone. I was real happy to get out of that field. Our supper was cold when we returned. Dave was cool about the cattle, too, said they would not have hurt us. All I know is that when they were real close to us, Dave was yelling and stoning them too.

The first trip we stopped at a K.O.A. at Alder, Montana. Virginia City was a few miles up from there. There was a pond left there from gold mining, Alder Gulch. There were a few huge trout in there just cruising around. Dave caught several on a nymph I tied. I netted one eight pound brown for him. Paul caught another brown about five or six pounds on an ant dry imitation. I came close and a pod swam near. The largest one veered over to my ant, rose, opened his mouth, and refused my fly. My hands shook awhile. That's as close as I came to a trophy. There were some big rainbows too, but we caught none of them.

Years later, my wife and I, and three youngest boys stopped at that same K.O.A. The owner had a fish nursery truck there, and stocked it with several hundred 10" trout. The big trout probably ate good until the small trout learned to hide.

My one son, Mark, found a wallet stuffed with money in the bathroom of that K.O.A. And he turned it in. The owner of it returned, identified the wallet, and gave my son a nice reward. I was really proud of Mark for his honesty. Later that trip, on the Gallatin River, I hooked a big rainbow on a dry fly, and jammed the rod in his hand. It took him a good while to land it, and it was the biggest trout of the trip. I enjoyed it as much as he did.

When we were camped at the Goose Creek campground on the Gallatin, our neighbors, the Fredricksons from Washington state, were retired and just traveling around. They kept the kids, David, 9; Joe, 12; and Mark, 14; in ice cream and Popsicles while we were there. Said the freezer needed to be emptied. (So they could refill it.) Mr. Fredrickson was a retired logger. He said, back in Washington, he used to "top" huge white cedars, about two feet in diameter where he topped them. He later bought the logging company. Once he went to Japan with those big logs to see what they did with them. White cedars are, I believe, about 40' long and 4-6' in diameter. The Japanese would bid on them at the dock, or a part of one, and would live off the products made from them for a year or more.

At Yellowstone, a day after Mark, Joe, and I hiked back to Clear Creek, about three miles with poor fishing. (The spawning run was over.) Mark and I did the same at Pelican Creek. Joe wouldn't go after he saw huge grizzly tracks in fresh mud at Clear Creek. We spooked a moose on the way in and got a peek at it. Then we got to Pelican Creek, but the run was over there also. We feasted on wild strawberries. I turned rocks over to check the bugs, and the stream was alive with them. I was admiring the scenery in this open area, and began wading across this twenty foot wide stream, when I heard a snort. Looking up, eyeball to eyeball ten feet away was mama and calf moose. I froze, looking for a tree to climb which wasn't there. Very slowly I waded backward out of the water, praying mama moose, being very protective, would not charge. Her hackles (mane) gradually settled down. I watched from a safe distance and noticed the hackles rise again when a coyote yelped from somewhere far off. They went back to grazing with the calf on the far side of mama.

While Mark and I were exploring, Rosalie and David hiked to a store with a Post Office several miles away. On their way back, this critter growled and hissed at them before gradually going into the woods. Rosalie described it to a ranger, who said, "Lady, you just faced the nastiest tempered animal in the park—a badger."

Later that same day, I came out of the restroom at Lake campground and almost walked into a bull bison, which earlier was farther away. I backtracked fast and waited until he left.

There might be people all around, but it's still the animals' home.

That was a great trip, and my wife was a good camper and helped with the driving too. When we left Montana, we headed to Houston, Texas, to visit my sister. Our first stop from Yellowstone was in Nebraska. When we got up early, the wind was howling and it was cold. I stuck my head in the door of the tent and said, "Do you want to eat breakfast here, or in the first McDonald's?" They had the tent down and properly put away before Rosalie and I finished up in the K.O.A. bathroom. They were learning teamwork early—and without supervision.

That was a three week trip. Hard to get three weeks in a row vacation in the summer at the Post Office.

Another trip there were five of us. Too many, but we made do. The worst part for me was the long drive. It was forty hours or more to the first camping spot on the Boulder River. I'm not a person that can doze off and rest while the truck is moving. Sometimes I could, on the way home when I was exhausted. Also, I usually rode shotgun with Walt M., who would immediately fall asleep after we switched and I drove. I couldn't doze when he was driving, because he had a tendency to fall asleep at the wheel. On another trip they claimed he made a short trip into a cornfield. On later trips, I refused to go unless the others agreed to an overnight stay in a motel on the way out and the way back. After they did that once, they never drove straight through again. On those early trips, you feel like a zombie for a day or two after being on the road for forty-plus hours.

Our daily evening meal was often fried fish, fried potatoes and onions, and buttered corn. On our trip with five, and whenever I drove my truck, I slept in the truck. One morning I was up when they were coming out of the tent. I swear I saw a green haze coming out of the tent. It's a good thing no one fired up a smoke before they aired that tent out. Another good reason to sleep in the truck was the snoring. Usually we were exhausted and slept after awhile. One guy snored so bad one time on the Gallatin that a tough motorcycle gang camped nearby left in the middle of the night. They were heard complaining, "How can anyone sleep with that noise all night?"

Many of the guys I fished with were school teachers, and they were usually a good influence on the kids at school. They had them fly-tying during some study halls, and a conservation club where they stocked fish and even raised some trout from eggs.

One year we met at a campground with three groups. One group was ten or more kids in one van. Eventually, they had disagreements and some flew home. All were not fishermen—and some, I think, just tired of the cramped conditions. Regardless, we had a group reunion. There may have been alcohol involved, but all had a good time and, prompted by a ranger, ended the evening with everyone singing "God Bless America."

You may have noticed there aren't too many fish stories in this section. Oh, we caught fish, but not in great amounts or sizes. Although fly fishing was the norm, one of the Walts (Walt H.) insisted we get a mess of sculpins (a minnow-type) where it was legal. We just murdered the trout with them and also caught big ones. I remember one I lost that I had on a long time. It was longer than a football and as big around. Finally, the hook just pulled out and the big brown sank out of sight. We only killed what we ate and released the big ones unless they were hooked bad and injured.

One year we were camped at a KOA at Boseman Hot Springs. An old Sioux woman there showed us how to go from the very hottest section to the coldest. It did some crazy things to your skin but it was really invigorating. While there, we stayed in a teepee, which was only a bit more expensive than the tent, and much larger. Also, there were foam mats—very comfy. Another couple from town was there. Bob went fishing with us while Cindy stayed at the campground. We went on a meat hunt and caught a mess next to the Ted Turner property which was posted. We could legally fish it as long as we stayed below the "high water" area. We grilled fish that evening dipped in "zesty Italian" salad oil. Delicious! I think Cindy ate more than any of us. Little girl, big appetite. We wondered if Bob didn't feed her.

On the Boulder River at Spring Creek Campground, we always did well. Not great, but well. We drove upstream one day to meet another gang. The fishing was underwhelming. Two of the group had their sons along (teenagers) and they were having a great trip. One thing they learned was "Loose lips sink ships." In other words, "Whatever happens in Montana, stays in Montana."

It was almost dark and the rain decided to pour down hard. "Guess what, guys," I said. "I believe the windows in the tent are open all the way."

"Oh no!! We'll be at the laundry all night trying to dry our sleeping bags," they lamented. But God was with us that day. We got within a half mile of camp and the road was completely dry. Such is the weather in the West.

Another year on the Boulder—same campground—we were about to sack out when a pair of beautiful young ladies were setting up camp right next to us. They were having trouble figuring out how to put their tent together, and Walt went zonkers trying to help them out. They weren't going to have anything to do with us old guys. Especially as ungroomed and stinky as we were. They stayed several days. Both were music majors at a California college. Early each morning, one would go downstream about a hundred yards and play her violin from a big flat rock near shore. She played beautifully, and kind of haunting too, as it was next to the bubbling water. I was going down the creek past her to fish one morning, and both were there and called me over to talk. Curious about fishing, they wanted me to take them both and teach them how to fish. I asked them if they had licenses or fishing gear and they had neither. I said, "You can walk along and I'll explain what I'm doing, but I don't have enough gear for both." They looked at how rugged the shoreline was down the river and declined. I didn't offer to drive them elsewhere on the river as most spots wouldn't be suitable to walk along in white gym shoes. Anyhow, they thanked me and wished me luck with the angling, and we both went on our ways.

When I got back to camp later, the guys wanted to know what the "honeys" wanted. I told them they preferred older, mature men and wanted personalized, guided fishing instruction in a wilderness setting. When I declined, they cried a bit, but accepted it. It really was kinda truthful, but the guys never quite believed me. Nevertheless, the girls never struck up a conversation with the "eager beaver" and I often let him know, even now, how I broke their hearts.

To sooth their feelings, another woman camped where the young sweeties had been. She was alone and her little car was jam-packed full of stuff, and I don't think it was all camping stuff. She was a bit older and kind of stayed to herself. We had a fish dinner that evening and invited her to join us. She did when we convinced her we had plenty. I think she really enjoyed the attention, and the food. Mostly the company. She reminded us of someone that was running away from a bad situation, and maybe we renewed her faith in other people. She never confided about her situation, but we liked to think we brightened her trip a little.

On a day trip to another section of the Boulder River, we parked the pickup and were looking over the water to decide if we wanted to fish there. These two beautiful, friendly horses trotted over to us. They had been eating some husks from someone's sweet corn roast. I actually did pet and put my arm around these beauties. My grandfather and also an uncle had horses, but they were plodding farm work horses. Another experience with horses was when I was trying to net some minnows on a small creek back in PA and these horses came. One took my hat in his teeth and ran off. I recovered the hat he dropped some yards off, and the playful horse tried to nip me with his teeth! That would have hurt. Anyhow, these two beautiful western horses hung around us 'til we opened some good cookies one of the wives sent along. They loved the cookies, but that was expensive and delicious horse food. I still have pictures of me and the horses.

Madison River was not my favorite river, mostly because I didn't catch many fish there, except in certain places. Near where a small stream came in, (West Madison?) was a small camping area. I crossed over the metal bridge one evening and caught several on wet flies, but this evening I wanted to catch a big one. Tying on two large stone nymphs and some extra weight, I cast into a deep pocket and it bounced along, and then a terrific hit. I set the hook and had a good tug of war with a lot of weight. After a long hard tussle, I brought the fish (plural!) to the top. It turned out it was two huge whitefish (not exactly what I was hoping for.) I cast into another deep pocket and tried again—another big whitefish. I went back to wets and settled for some small 'bows and that was fine.

Later years, it seemed like a float with a guide and customers came down every five minutes and fished all the wade-able targets. It got very frustrating.

Well, one year I brought my float tube, (or belly-boat,) and fished Quake Lake, on the Madison river, just a few miles upriver. That was weird, fishing over sunken treetops, thinking about the people under me that got caught when the quake hit and either drowned or covered up with the mountain that fell over the river and blocked it and made the lake. Occasionally my feet would hit the top of an underwater tree and I'd almost jump out of my waders. I actually caught several nice rainbows, mostly by trolling a wet fly or casting near fish feeding on top. An eagle scolded me when I got got too close to its aerie. Neat!

When we stopped at the store/Post Office/gas station, I asked the man to fill the tube with air and he obliged saying, "Bring it around the back where I have a compressor." This garage/store/P.O. (they only had mail go out two times a week) was just a mile or three below where the quake shook the mountain across the river and across part of the gap. As I walked down to the back of the building I noticed the Madison in the background. As he started the small compressor and I got the float tube ready to receive the air, I asked the man, "Were you living here when the quake hit?"

"Yeah . . . I was." In a drawl similar to a Texan.

"Did it shake you out of bed?"

"No. It didn't." Slowly he replied.

"Well, when did you know it hit?"

The man said, "Well, every morning when I get up, I go to the kitchen and get a drink of water. I got my water and looked out of the window and the river was dry." Very serious-like he said, "Right then and there I knew something was wrong."

I looked at him closely to see if he was pulling my leg, but he was dead serious! Either he was the world's soundest sleeper, or the quake seriously rattled his brain. I didn't even bother asking his wife when I returned to the store. I'm not sure I wanted to hear her answer.

The year some of us went to Kelley Creek was a fruitless adventure. It was the only time we fished in Idaho, except for several jaunts to the Snake River at Harriman's Railroad Ranch. This was an hour or so from the Madison River. The big ones were hard to fool on tricots, a size 22 or 24 hook. The other guys were up—and downstream, and I was fishing just below the bridge that went over to the ranch. The morning hatch was over, and I was using a small hopper or large caddis. (The way I tied, it was hard to tell the difference.) Wouldn't you know, it was a beautiful 20" rainbow that took my fly. I was up to my wader tops and trying to take a picture of it, and I heard, "That's a nice fish." I glanced toward the near bank and this very attractive, well-dressed woman was watching me. I thanked her for the compliment and wondered where she came from. It was a half mile walk from the parking area across the highway. I put the disposable camera back in my vest and later got it soaked. The big trout pictures didn't come out.

Later, at home, I was watching television and it showed Winston Churchill and Lady Churchill, his daughter who married Averil Harriman, a former Secretary of State from a wealthy family. I yelled, "That's the woman! That's her!!"

My wife, Rosalie, unruffled, said, "What's the matter with you? What are you yelling about?"

I explained about the woman at the Harriman Ranch.

"Yeah, right!" she replied. "And Clark Gable visited me while you were gone, too."

I think I convinced her years later who the lady really was.

Getting back to Kelley Creek, we went over the LoLo Pass and prayed we didn't get any big lumber trucks coming at us on the winding dirt road. Finally, after a long, dusty trip, we came to the beautiful Kelley Creek, and near a ranger's home, we checked a huge cedar. Four of us could barely reach around it by joining our hands. We finally reached the state campground. Each campsite was surrounded with some high berry bushes of some type. There were hummingbirds around everywhere. We got the tent set up, ate a bite, and went fishing. Wild Bill and I went upriver and Ardie and Walt went down. We noticed our spot by a swinging bridge and I went up near a small waterfall coming down off a steep hill. I was lucky enough to get two cutthroats and Wild Bill caught some whitefish under the bridge.

Did I mention we were going through a very hot stretch of weather? Over 100F for more than two straight weeks. The other guys got no trout. The next evening (it was too hot during the day) Bill and I switched. He fished near the waterfall and got some cutts and I got whitefish. The others got none and probably the heat made them give up. After reading about Kelley Creek for years, we figured the writers were all liars. The truth was that cutthroat trout just can't handle the hot water. They probably found springs and cold deep spots and just survived the hot stretch of weather. I've seen the same thing on Penn's Creek, and have pictures of hundreds of brown trout ganged up where cold, oxygenated streams entered. They sure weren't in a feeding mood. A friend, Walt M., and I got a pump and sprayed cold water over them for two days. Different people walked along the creek and counted as many as fifty-some dead trout that they could see.

Enough survived on Penn's that year and the stream healed up. A natural occurrence? From century to century it may happen several times. I've seen it happen three times in the last few years. _Not always_ as severe as it was was in August of '99. I'll blame it on the population and business explosion, and drilling more wells and taking too much water out of the aquifer.

Back to Kelley Creek, it was so hot, and no relief in sight, that we just sat in lawn chairs drinking Kool Aid and munching on beef jerky. In our shorts, of course. We cut the Idaho trip short and went to the other side of the Divide.

Another year, Jim, Reed and I went out with a back country trip in Yellowstone. After getting all the necessary permits, we got a boat ride across Yellowstone Lake to Beaverdam Creek. The water was low that year too, and we had to backpack an extra three miles with all our gear, including tent, food, and fishing equipment. We caught a bunch of cutthroat trout the first day, and after seeing all those flies, got tough the second day like a brown trout. Then we hiked to the Yellowstone where it comes into the lake. Grizzly country! We had no problem, but several years later, at Heart Lake, a grizzly went in a tent and killed a young couple. This was only a few miles away. We saw lots of moose there, but no bears.

While we were at Beaverdam Creek camp, a horse group came through with beautiful horses and a bunch of tourists—also a cute young cowgirl that was the wrangler in charge of the horses. Some of the horses were giving her a rough time and she cursed them out and whipped them enough to make me blush and be afraid of her. There was a wild storm approaching and they decided to move. One of the main cowboys was afraid the horses would get in "the Yellowstone bog" (as he called it) and break a leg.

Thank God they left. Twenty horses can make a big stink, and draw a bunch of flies, and maybe bears. We were making our supper—freeze-dried meals rehydrated with boiling water. Just before Reed finished, the storm struck and it was wild in that back country. My dinner was beef and potatoes and it was quite good. Reed got about half wet, rushing the meals into the tent. We wondered how the horse train made out. They were headed along the edge of the lake on the mountain side, and we didn't know how they could set up any protection from the storm before it hit them. I'll bet the young cowgirl was really cursing when the rain and wind reached them.

One year, a group of us was heading home and we needed gasoline really bad. If we didn't get any soon, even on I-90, we'd have to park the truck 'til things opened up in the morning. Watching the gas gauge in South Dakota and worrying we wouldn't get home in time (family and work awaited) with a lay-over, we started seeing tents, campers, and people on the medial strip. Then, after five or six miles of campers, we came to Sturgis, SD. Guess what? It was the Harley-Davidson convention. Thousands of people in the middle of nowhere. What a circus! And this at 3AM! We were lucky enough to get gasoline and get out in a short time.

Bob was another teacher friend of mine who had a camp near mine. Bob helped coach wrestling and loved to explore when we were out west. After retiring, he worked with an outfitter in Montana, guiding and wrangling. His fellow coach said he always wanted to be a cowboy. Tough and in shape, he had lost his wife just before retiring, and his kids were now adults, so this was a good way for him to spend some time. One summer he was taking supplies to the wilderness camp for the outfitter, and the horses started to act up. As he didn't want to let any get loose and have to round them up, he had the reins wrapped around his hand. One horse pulled so hard he pinched the tips of several fingers off Bob's hand. After getting to the camp, they wanted him to go to a hospital or doctor to get it attended to. Being practical, he refused, as the nearest help was many miles away—maybe two days or more. They fixed him up as best they could with their first aid kit, and he never had any problems.

His group was at Rock Creek one time and this twit and his dog "Orvis" was fishing near Bob. The man was outfitted from head to toe with Orvis, Patagonia, Columbia—latest high tech gear—and his dog, Orvis, was running wild, jumping in and out of the water, trying to catch Bob's fly line, and just being a pest. The man would call Orvis from time to time, with no authority, and of course the dog did what he wanted. Bob, being very patient, eventually had enough. He reeled in his line, leaned it against a bush, walked down to the twit and got right in his face.

"Listen, you drip. You either get Orvis under control or both of you are going to get the L.L. Bean!"

The man obviously wasn't going to argue with Bob, and quickly rounded up Orvis and disappeared.

CHAPTER EIGHT—OTHER TRIPS

My first trip to Canada, I was one year out of high school, and my partner "Mouse" had another year. We stopped at a hardware store partway up into Ontario, bought our licenses, and asked where was a good place to fish. The storekeeper grinned, knowing we were innocents. He kindly directed us to a small lake called Pope Lake, We got permission from a Mr. Pope, who the lake was probably named for. We asked where we could camp. "Right down over the hill—there's a spring and a nice grassy spot." We set up the tent, then decided we needed a mattress, so we drove up the road, pulled off, went into the woods and cut a bunch of spruce boughs. It softened up the ground a bit and smelled fresh. It may have helped keep mosquitoes away too. We made a cooler by putting a big empty lard can in the spring, and weighted it down with a rock in the bottom. We went back up to Mr. Pope, who had a little store, and bought milk, bread, eggs, butter, and maybe lunch meat. We probably had canned soup and Dinty Moore stew also. We were easy to please. Mouse would get up early and jog a few miles then to stay in shape for football and wrestling. He was good at both and later got a scholarship to Arkansas U. The lake spilled out into a small stream nearby, and at night we'd take some nice bass with jitterbugs. We didn't get much during the day, so Mouse caught some frogs, hooked them in the back legs, and that got some more. We rented an old wooden rowboat, but got most of the nice fish near our camp. One night we were up the lake and I got a walleye on the surface with a "crazy-crawler." I never heard of catching them on the surface before.

We had a bunch of fish on the chain stringer hanging off the side of the boat one morning. While eating a sandwich for lunch, we noticed that the fish on the stringer were really active. We decided, since they were so lively, we wouldn't clean them 'til supper. They *were* supper. Wrong! They were lunch, but not for us. We decided to go for a boat ride (no motor here, just oars) so we popped the fish in the boat and gaped. There was only one and a half bass there. No pike, no other bass. All that jiggling around must have been a big turtle helping himself. I don't know what else could have done it, and never had that happen before or since.

It was a good trip and we did well, both camping and fishing, despite no experience or planning.

Later, I went with another group to the Mississippi River (no, not the big one) in Ontario near where Mouse and I fished. The small river (creek) would flow between small lakes for miles, and we caught some bass, small pike, and even some walleyes downlake near a hydro dam which was blocked off by floating logs chained together. I was just above there, alone, one black night, casting a jitterbug where we caught some bass before. A beaver (I think!) made a splash that just about gave me heart failure. I'm not usually jumpy, but I sure wasn't prepared for that.

Another time, two of the fellows were fishing down the small lake a ways off, and for some reason, I was alone in my aluminum pram. I was fishing around stumps and lily pads, when this storm came up fast and furious. Naturally, I waited 'til the last second and was cranking in a foot long bass when the wall of hard rain came. I plopped the bass in the pram, threw my poncho over my head, and kicked the motor on. It decided to go full speed and smash into a hollow log and stall after about ten feet, which knocked me off the seat with the poncho over my head. The boat was only 12 feet and narrow. When I went off the seat I fell against the side and water poured in. I struggled to keep it upright, but finally lost to gravity and tilted sideways. Me and all my gear went in the drink. Fortunately, it was warm and only shoulder-deep. Naturally, my tackle box was open and metal, so it sank too. The boat didn't sink because of styrofoam under the seats, but all the water made it unstable. As usual I was good in bad crises, probably because I was good at putting myself in bad situations, and got a lot of practice. I took the anchor rope, which was around my legs, and tied it to my floating boat seat for a marker. Then, emptying the water from the boat as best I could, I started diving down and retrieving my gear. By the time my buddies arrived from down the lake, I had everything but two boxes of split shot off the bottom and I was in the boat, ready to go to the dock and dry everything off. They, grinning, had heard me yelling, and wondered why my other boat cushion and water jug were floating down their way. For once, I didn't have a smart-ass answer for them.

Other potential dangers included (I wasn't involved) throwing gasoline in the wood cookstove to perk up the fire. One guy did a really neat dance across the room beating out flames on himself and the floor. Another fellow, deathly afraid of lightening, nearly had a heart attack running up a steep hill to the cabin from the boat dock. Being a chain smoker, overweight and out-of-shape didn't help. When two fellows went to Mrs. White's (the landlady) to pay rent, and to the store for things, we decided to play a little trick. This was now after dark. Chumming a big raccoon onto the screened-in porch for food, we had a rope tied to the porch door. When he was in the porch, we closed the inside door and pulled the rope and closed the porch door. The coon forgot all about the food and climbed every bit of the screen looking for a way out, and making angry noises. We were afraid it would tear the screen apart and we didn't want to have to pay for any damages, so when the coon was on the other side of the porch, Don dashed to the screen door and quick propped it open with a broom. It didn't take long for the critter to get out. It would have been fun to watch if we had let things go 'til they came back.

There was an outboard motor/car repair place nearby. A sign stated that labor was five dollars an hour, "ten if you watch, twenty if you help." The owner said that eliminated a lot of problems.

Mrs. White lived near there. There was a rain barrel on our camp (her original home) and she would come to get soft water from the barrel to wash her hair. She told us she wanted to have someone to build her two more boats and another cabin, but she couldn't find anyone. "Up here," she said, "they're either too busy, too lazy, or too dumb." That could have been many places in this old world.

Getting bored with the civilized fishing, we decided to go to the far North. This one neighbor that had a radiator shop nearby had been going to our target lake for a few years, and we started pestering him for information about the place. After a while word got back to us that he'd be damned if he'd baby-sit us. (We were both booked for the same week.) Well, we got there before he did, as they had to get more beer to replace what they drank on the way up. After several days, me and Don (who did little fishing back home) came back to the cabin area again with several huge northern pike. As we tried to clean these two big pike, two older fellows were watching us do a really bad job, and we overheard them grumbling as they watched us: "They can catch them but can't clean them. We can clean them but can't catch them." That really tickled Don.

Later we learned to fillet walleyes, which were much tastier and easier to clean. The huge, toothy pike were, at that time, nicer trophies, and that's what impressed us then. As the week went on, we learned the lake better and came back one evening with a nice catch. One of the beer drinking gang from home that I knew well came over, bleary-eyed, and complimented us on the catch.

"Hell," he said, "all our guys want to do is drink. We just troll and *hope* we catch fish. I can drink at home. I want to catch some fish!"

The whole way around the three sides of their screened-in porch was stacked four-high with beer cans. Also, we could always tell where they were on the lake by the trail of discarded empties. We never went North at the same time as those guys again.

The dirt road to this lake was a four hour trip with, preferably, a high-off-the-ground pick-up truck. The road, which was described on the brochure as a good gravel road to the lodge, was really a very rough road sixty—or seventy-some miles. We got a laugh one time on the way up when we came to a spot where it was washed out with water flowing through it, typical of many like it. Someone put a sign up that said, "Caution—Walleye Crossing—PA Fish Commission."

We got the bright idea of hiring a cook one time. This guy that worked at a nearby gas station said he'd go and cook—"just pay my way—no wages." We couldn't afford it any other way. We knew he was no chef from the Waldorf Astoria, but he was really dumb. Knowing this, a friend that was a good cook patiently instructed him how to cook a really nice 10 lb. rolled rump roast. Unfortunately the instructor couldn't go on the trip. Well, the night came when the beef was to be supper. We were all apprehensive, wondering if the guy could even read. Six of us came dragging in about six o'clock, hungry.

"How's the roast?" we asked.

"I must have done something wrong," said the cook. "I boiled it four or five hours and it's still not tender."

My peanut butter and jelly sandwiches were delicious that night.

An early trip one year, Merle and I decided to explore a bit to a little known trout lake. I was a bit skittish about getting separated back one of those remote trails that weren't marked all that well. I brought whistles along because you can hear them a lot farther than you can yell. I saw this tip in an outdoor magazine, and thought it could be better-used in boats, because you just don't hike much in the thick, boggy north woods of Quebec. We found what we thought was the correct creek and area several miles from our vehicle. Merle insisted on following the stream up a few miles, and I decided to fish the stream.

"Don't get carried away and get lost. We can't get a search party up like in Pennsylvania."

Merle was a real hard head and you couldn't tell him anything.

Finally I caught a small brookie, so at least I knew we were in the right area. Several hours passed and nothing from Merle. I blew my whistle long and loud a few blasts, waited, and no answer. I did this every fifteen to twenty minutes for several hours more and nothing. The end of the day was approaching and I was beginning to get concerned. I knew I could find my way back to the car, so I didn't want to go from the area and get lost myself. The car, also, was on an obscure logging trail, a mile or more from the main dirt road.

I was just about at my wit's end when I finally heard some thrashing in the brush. Merle was nearing me, looking a bit wild-eyed yet relieved.

"Why didn't you answer my whistle blasts? I've been blowing my lungs out every fifteen or twenty minutes."

"Mine wouldn't work," he said. "Must have gotten clogged with dirt or something. Besides, I just heard you about ten minutes or so; the wind was blowing and that's why I couldn't hear you."

Later, he admitted he'd gotten "turned around" and disoriented. He did find the lake, but couldn't approach it to fish because of all the bog and brush near it. He said it would have been rough to get even a boat or canoe there. If there were any decent trout in that lake, they were well protected by the terrain.

Trying my fly rod one day for walleye was fruitless, but I did catch a lake whitefish about sixteen or eighteen inches. I chuckled, and was about to toss him back in when Don said, "No! I want that big guy for bait." I put the fish in the bait bucket and we went to another spot. Don actually did use that whitefish, which we called a "chub." Getting a big five-aught treble hook from one of the guys, he put it behind the dorsal fin with wire leader. He used two baseball-sized bobbers on because the bait pulled one under. It was too heavy to cast, so he put it overboard where he wanted it, opened the bail, and we let the wind blow the boat off a ways, then anchored. Let him have his fun, I thought.

After about forty-five minutes, the big bobbers jiggled a bit and *POW!!* It went under like a submarine caught it. He let it under for about five minutes, then reeled in the slack and struck several times. A big fish showed lots of power, went in one direction and then another. We pulled up anchor and the motor, so nothing would snag when the huge pike got close. Well, the monster made a pass directly under me near the surface. Its head was 10-11" wide at least and he must have been six feet long.

"Do you want me to follow him, Don?" (After it made another long run.)

"No, I want him to get tired."

That didn't work. The fish turned on a right angle, and with the force of the fish against all that line in the water, broke it off at the rod tip. Very disappointed, we went over it, second-guessed the strategy: the line was defective, too much line out, should have followed him, should have put more pressure on the fish (10 lb. test on spinning gear.) Maybe one or all of these may have worked, but I have my doubts. It was a truly large pike and we all got a good close-up look at it—probably record size. We had a big net, but I'm not sure we could have got it in close enough to boat it. I don't think I would have wanted a six foot long pike with a huge mouth full of razor-sharp teeth flopping around in a 14' boat, knocking over tackle boxes and fishing rods. It would have been a circus to find out and and live through it, though. It was a thrill as it was.

Several days later, we were fishing the same area when a boat nearby, with people from a town near us, hooked what appeared to be a big one. They were motoring near us, following the fish, and as they approached, we asked if he was really big. They didn't answer by voice—their mouths agape as they watched the big pike put it in another gear. The man's drag on his reel couldn't keep up with the line hissing out. Then it popped like a rifle shot. They just stared with their jaws open.

I said to Don, "What do you wanta bet that was the same fish?"

We never hooked any more pike that even approached that size again, although on a later trip, when the other guys went to a different lake, I was on a side stream between two parts of the lake trying to catch some bait fish, and I saw in the clear, shallow water several pike cruising by. None were more than about forty inches, until one about five feet long came by, and actually stopped and looked right at me, then resumed his trip. I grabbed another rod with a big Rapala on it, but the fish ignored it. That was a spooky feeling.

That evening when I returned, the camp was lit up and the porch was dark. I could hear giggling inside and I knew there were no girls there, so I knew they were up to something. Slowly I approached the door. They had a lynx that one of the men had shot that day propped up to scare me. I gave them a sound cursing and we exchanged stories of the day over a great meal of fried walleye with fried potatoes and onions.

Wild Bill and I were motoring up the lake one day and we saw mama moose with a calf in the water off a point of land, feeding. Getting his movie camera ready for me, Bill wanted me to roll the film as he got closer. I could only see through the view-finder and warned him not to get too close. Naturally, he did anyway, and when I looked, all I could see was moose fuzz.

"Whip the boat around!" Bill just laughed, but we were close, and I know how fast those long-legged animals can move, even in water.

On another side trip one day, we had boats loaded on the truck and one of the guys, Elwood, had his rifle along in case we saw a bear. There were rabbits (probably snowshoe rabbits) every few hundred feet, and Elwood decided to shoot one for supper. At fifty feet, he finally hit one after five shots, and almost tore it in two pieces. It was still alive and the poor thing was dragging the rear half, which was hanging by a string of fur. After several more shots it was mercifully dead. The "Great White Hunter" said the rifle was sighted in for a hundred yards, but we didn't let up on him the whole trip. There wasn't enough meat on that bunny for a small cat after he was through with it.

Elwood and I did house painting on the side to pay for fishing trips, and he was good at that. He was too nice a guy for our trips, though, because he was an easy target. He got some revenge by being a sound sleeper and a loud snorer.

Don was a bit unorthodox, as you noticed with the huge whitefish as pike bait. As small suckers which we got from a small stream were scarce, they were legal because they were from the same watershed area. Later Don used hot dogs. No luck. Then he used bacon, which he actually did get a three foot long Northern pike on. We were afraid he was going to empty our coolers of human food if we didn't stop him. Fortunately, he finally realized he could catch more on artificials than with the type of bait under bobbers he was using. It did take more effort, though.

There were usually larger groups on these trips and that caused a problem with cooking. Most of these people couldn't cook, and the ones that could got roped into a lot of extra work. The water had to be heated for dishwashing, and of course, there were always a few that expected the others to do things for them.

Then, there was the problem of snoring. This was serious. Several of us were hurting because of lack of sleep. The year there were ten of us, it got so bad that one fellow spent a lot of time tape-recording people snoring throughout the night. During the family fish fry when we returned, he played the tape for entertainment. It got a lot of laughs then, but it wasn't funny at the time for the light sleepers. I now keep earplugs in my kit.

Later, we graduated to some fly-in trips to the Gouin Reservoir, which was a huge impoundment in Quebec. Different out-fitters leased out different areas from the Indians or government, I was never quite sure which.

The first trip was with an outfitter that tried to squeeze the most people in. We signed up for a more remote camp that was not too ritzy. The dock was a disaster and the outhouse leaned on a sharp angle. We thought seriously of propping it up on one side with saplings, but we had no tools. Every morning, the critters under the camp were busy gnawing on the flooring. There was an ancient gas refrigerator and a gas grill. Our group of four enjoyed the trip. My son, Mark, was the cook, and we enjoyed many great walleye meals.

The French-Canadian pilots were a group of a different type. I don't know if they were fatalists or comedians. During the regulation safety talk, our pilot finished up with, "In case there are any survivors, the life vests are under the seats." (Which couldn't be reached in the tough de Havilland Beaver plane, because we were so jammed with gear, plus five of us tightly packed in the seats.)

On a later trip with a different, more caring, out-fitter, we went to the same area of the Reservoir. We had a much nicer cabin with a better dock—even though that year, the water was higher and the dock was semi-underwater. The outfitter's younger sister, Julie, also flew, and in the middle of the week the cute Julie flew to our camp. Wearing her big lumberjack boots, all ninety pounds of her got a sixty pound container of gas mix for the outboard motors, and a propane tank out of the plane, down the ladder to the pontoons, across the wet bouncing dock to the shore, without any help from us. (Partially because we'd have put too much weight on the wet, tilting dock.) Little Julie could handle it all, including flying in a vast wilderness area alone. When she was done, we offered her coffee, but she said in her French accent that she had too many more stops. I asked her how old she was.

She replied, "Almost 18."

I said, "Hell, I got underwear older than that."

She understood my U.S. English and got a big laugh.

We often wondered about her safety with strangers in those wild woods. But when you think about it, any stupid moves by a drunk or horny fisherman, and they could just strand him there, never to be found again.

There was a fairly young, retired man that spent the summers working for "Tamarac," our outfitter, for a few years as guide, handyman, etc., just for expenses. He was from Lewisburg, and at that time he actually lived next door to a friend I grew up with and played ball with. I don't know what he did for a living and he made it somewhat of a mystery. Regardless, he was guiding a Dutch official and family, as a reward of some type. It seems there were drugs being dropped off by plane in this lake, recovered, and buried before being transferred for distribution and sale. I gathered the Dutch man was a lawyer or some connection to the prosecution. One of the druggers was caught under a tarp, trying to escape in some local's pick-up

truck in a small logging town by name of Clova. I think our handyman/
guide wanted us to think he had something to do with the break-up of
the drug ring, without actually saying it. Was he a "narc" of some type
that worked in cooperation with Canada? I'll never really know. The only
fed connection I know of near Lewisburg is the federal prison. Bucknell
University is there also.

Rain most always was a part of our trips, so we always went with proper
rain gear. It also had a lot to do with flying in or out.

It was necessary for Tamarac to contract another plane one year through
Air Melancon, because Tamarac was in the process of buying another de
Havilland Beaver—the work horse of the north woods. They hadn't made
any new ones since the 1960's, so people kept rebuilding old ones.

We arrived at their dock, or waterport, whatever you'd call an airport
for pontoon-type planes. We were on time, and they had several Beavers
lined up along the dock. There was a big set of scales there and we were
allowed one hundred twenty pounds per person, including fishing gear,
etc. There was an overall allowance of the total weight limit, and, including
a case of Molson Blue, we came within a couple pounds of it. We teased
Big Walt that it was a good thing he only packed one set of underwear.

It was raining and we were getting impatient to get going. Finally we
took off, and the rain poured off the windshield. I noticed the pilot, who
was built like a gorilla, was staying below the cloud cover and by-passing
all the high places in the otherwise flat country. Of course there were lakes
everywhere up there. After about a half hour we went back to Air Melancon,
because after listening to all the radio jabber, he decided it wasn't safe. It
was only another half hour to our target—I guess it really wasn't safe. Or
he didn't want to spend the night at our camp, or he was afraid he'd have to
set down on some remote lake, or he had a date that night (with a female
gorilla.)

After waiting several more hours, the rain still coming down and us
getting restless, the pilot decided to try again. I couldn't see that the rain
had lessened, and I couldn't understand the French jabber on the radio, but
we finally got there safely and the pilot left after we got unloaded. He must
have got back OK because he was the same pilot to pick us up at the end of

the week. The big, hefty, hairy pilot had a good touch and knew his trade wasn't without risks, but didn't take crazy chances. A small town named Clova, where the drug dealer got caught under the tarp, was nearby, a half hour as the crow, or airplane, flies. Clova was used as mid-week quarters for Tamarac's pilots. Our dock was falling apart, and the teenaged pilot (not Julie) stripped to his shorts, dove in the water, and did a so-so job on our dock. He had to have been in the water at least an hour and I knew it was cold. He didn't seem to mind it at all. We took a lake bath our first fly-in trip and damn near froze. Later, I brought a solar shower and it was a big hit. They actually work. Tamarac has since installed hot water (propane) showers at most of his cabins. Big hit also, but more money.

I had these old blue plaid polyester pants I always brought on these trips because they were too ugly to wear at home. They flared at the bottom like bell bottoms, but were so comfy I hated to dump them. One trip I stained them so we had a regular funeral for them. My so-called friends urged me strongly, so with cameras and tears rolling, I gave a short speech, tied a knot in one pantleg, dropped a softball-sized rock in, and twirled them and let go. They fluttered beautifully and the long flight landed with a plunk.

We often wondered what people would think if they ever hooked them some day. I don't think that polyester would rot or disintegrate.

The cabins at Gouin Reservoir were scattered over many square miles of the lake. Also, there were other outfitters with their own leases with camps scattered over the area. Several private camps were mixed in, and there was at least one Indian home I knew of too. Somehow, they all—Indians, government, outfitters, private owners—made it work. Maybe not always smoothly, but I think the bottom line is, Money Talks!

One dark and stormy night, after we got back to camp, we ate, played some cards, then went to bed. The storm hit very hard, the wind shaking the cabin and the rain pelting the windows. Then Walter, with the touchy stomach, got out of bed in a rush, dumped another person's clothes and other personals all over the floor, charged onto the porch to the leeward side and took care of his sanitary business with everyone cursing him for the disturbance, stealing the cardboard box, and doing this on the porch (and me just laughing.) They wanted to know why he didn't run to the out house.

"Couldn't find my flashlight, didn't want to get wet, and besides, I didn't have time before the 'blowout!'"

Walter got soaked on the porch anyhow, and the next day took the soggy, yuchy box and got rid of it deep in the woods.

We found out the next year that the same storm blew a roof off a camp we had stayed at another year. There were six people in there at the time, and luckily no one was hurt. They were also lucky that there was another cabin beside theirs that was vacant, so they gathered their wet belongings and moved to the next camp. It could have been a real disaster, but instead became a great adventure they could tell their families and friends about when they got home.

We brought two-way walkie talkies with us that year, and Walt and I were in one boat, not catching many. Worse, the wind was vicious. We called Bill and the other Walt (I have a lot of friends with the same first name) and asked, "How're you making out?"

Excitedly they replied, "We're really into the walleyes."

"How's the wind there?" and "Where are you?" we shot back.

"On the far side, near some pine trees and white birch trees, and there's rocks along the shore."

That describes every shore line in every lake in all of Canada. They were leaving for lunch when we finally located them several miles away. The Walt I was with and I did catch a lot of walleyes that day. We would drift through the "hot spot" with twister jigs bouncing the bottom. Virtually every drift we caught several each. They really did find a great spot. Finally sated, we headed back to eat.

CHAPTER NINE—MORE EXPLORING

BWCA, or Boundary Water Canoe Area

My nephew Bill had many trips logged to BWCA since he was a Boy Scout. He talked me into going there, and I was convinced once I found out that we'd get to a good bass lake of which there were hundreds there. There were six of us this first trip, and the only way to travel once we got in the park was by canoe. No motors, no canned goods, camping in designated areas only, this area, which included Quetico Park in Canada above Minnesota, covered as large an area as several small eastern states.

We flew to Duluth and the outfitter drove us to Ely, Minnesota, to a campground where we stayed overnight. The next day we were driven to Crane Lake where we, with our three canoes and another group with two canoes, were loaded onto a motorized boat. We stopped at a ranger station where we got our Canadian licenses and permits, then we were delivered to where we unloaded and got into our canoes with all our gear.

From there we were on our own for a week with freeze-dried food and some fresh meat and eggs for three of the days, packed in a hard insulated pack. After a long but scenic paddle of about six hours, we had a lunch break of peanut butter and jelly sandwiches and KoolAde. We got to the site after six portages—up to a mile each new lake. Bill and Sam Smart (yes, that's his real name) were the veterans, and I was with Sam. He was a little guy but in good shape. I carried the canoe on one portage, but I had trouble with it, so even though the Duluth packs were much heavier—sixty to seventy pounds—I found them easier than carrying the clumsy canoe, even though they were Kevlar and only weighed about forty pounds.

Finally, Bill, Bill Jr., Sam, myself, Harley, and Shane got set up in camp, ate, and watched the sun set. There were two tents and I elected to sleep with Bill and Bill Jr. (Billy) because the two big guys (Harley was 6'6" or more) really snored loud. Seriously. Ear plugs became standard equipment in my medicine kit and still is to this day.

Roland Martin fished this same lake (on TV) and the egoist claimed the lake was named after him. Wrong!

It was, I believe, the first full week in June and it was so hot several days I slept in nothing but my undershorts, even with the tent screens open all the way. Two years later, during that same week, we had an afternoon snowstorm. If you don't like the weather in Quetico, just wait; it'll change soon. Nevertheless, the smallmouth bass fishing was great.

The lakes are among the oldest in the world and are, according to electronic gear, flat as a pancake after you get away from the edge of the shore, from many thousands of years of dirt and debris settling. Bill and Sam, after reading how to do it, trolled a spinner and worm or twister on the bottom, with the canoe of course, and caught several 20" size lake trout out in the flat part of the lake.

I brought my fly rod, of course, and Sam said he'd show me where I could get some easily. He insisted I use popping bugs, which weren't too successful that early in the year. After going a hundred yards or so in this prime water, I talked Sam into my using a big black woolly bugger. This, to me, would be a great imitation for a leech, which was a popular live bait for bass in that region. He reluctantly agreed, and I just tore them up until he could stand it no longer, and picked up his spinning rod. Not being safe to cast the fly rod any longer, I put it away so we could both fish. What a blast! Later, just to prove my point to Sam, I tied a black woolly bugger behind a surface plug, on a two-foot dropper. They ignored the surface lure, and still whacked the leech imitation regularly.

Within a few years, Bill and Sam were also hooked on fly fishing for trout, even though they lived in Fredricksburg, VA. Bill makes four to eight trips to PA each year to fish for trout.

In Quetico, the second year, after the snow storm, Sam was up early and woke us with, "Boys, we got a problem." We got up and he showed us where a bear had somehow got our foam cooler from where we had it hoisted up off a tree limb. "What all did he get?" I asked. The foam cooler had two packs of cheese and summer sausage, maybe some other stuff.

"There he is yet! Up on the hill!" Sam yelled.

I said, "I'll get our stuff back from that damn thief."

"Don't be crazy," Sam said.

"I see more black bear at my camp in PA in a week than you'll see up here in a year. If I see a threatening move, I'll back off," I said, "but they're not grizzlies."

I went up and shooed the good-sized black bear away, but only retrieved one sausage and a pack of cheese slices. He broke the cooler and ate the rest. I didn't want to, but Sam wouldn't rest until we moved camp, which took a big part of the day. I felt we still had as much chance of a bear at the new site as the old one.

Billy, Jr. and I fished together most of our second trip, when there were just four of us, although I shared the tent with Sam.

The weather, as I said, turned crappy that week, and although there was no more snow, the wind got really bad sometimes. Billy and I still had a good time several days. The one time, the wind funneled to our protected spot and the bass were stacked and hungry. I was fishing odor injected plastic leeches and it was like fishing live helgramites at home. They'd just pick it up and swim with it. Billy couldn't figure out how I was catching them without bending my rod.

"Just pretend it's live bait and watch your line."

He soon caught on and put on a clinic for me. The kid just loved fishing and was equally good at hunting. The only trouble was trying to anchor the canoe and hold position with rocks as make-shift anchors.

That same day, we went back to eat and to try some areas protected from the wind that were nearby. There was a short portage leading to a hot spot in the lake just above. Where the stream from the lake above entered the portage, we started to catch a bunch of hefty smallies off a hump under the surface of the water. It seemed every time we'd pass a black or smoke-colored twister over that hump, we'd have a smashing strike. The wind was relentless though, and we tired of trying to hold the canoe in position.

We took our canoe over the 100 foot portage and fished there for awhile. Bill and Sam had taken a side trip to another lake that day in the wind. They were fearless in a canoe in rough water, but not when there's a bear around.

Billy and I could see the wind was getting really nasty even on the semi protected area where we were. We pulled the canoe completely out of the lake and we got our backs against a steep bank on the lee side and hoped no trees got blown over us. The wind was that strong. We waited it out and made the short trip to camp. No damage we could see, but Sam and Bill weren't back yet, though it was not late yet. Soon they made it back. They had pulled in during the hard blow, too. It wasn't an ideal place, but Bill had a touch of the runs, so they pulled in and went into the woods a piece as it hit hard then. They also hoped no trees fell on them.

As it turned out, when we got out and home we found out how serious the storm was. Bill gets a magazine about the area, and read that that storm blocked many of the portages with downed trees. As it turned out, it took several years with chainsaws to clear the most used passages. As far as I knew, there were no serious injuries.

The second year, I decided not to drive down to Virginia and fly out of Dulles airport with them. I got a flight from State College to Duluth, and they got a flight to Minneapolis and rented a car and met me at Duluth. When the plane dropped down to land, we entered the thickest pea soup fog I even saw in my life. It kept dropping down and I knew they were going to land with instruments. I was even more scared than when in the service, going from Guam to the Philippines, we were half way and two of the six engines started smoking and they feathered them. It was a MAT—military air transport—Constellation with six motors, as I remember. We came back to Guam and they worked on the motors for six hours. We got back on the same airplane and made the flight to Clark Field in the Philippines. Did I mention that on the second try, we flew through a typhoon? Scary, especially when it looked like lightning going through the cabin and felt like the bottom dropped out a few times.

Well, back in the USA, the plane landed safely at Duluth and I couldn't see the airport building, the fog was that thick. We made it there, and Sam said he couldn't believe the plane would try to land.

"You should have been on the plane!" I said with my voice quivering. "I'll be back soon, I gotta go to the men's room."

Thank God for good pilots!

Alberta, British Columbia, Colorado

After talking to people that had been there, I decided, in self pity, that I should go and experience some good fly fishing. The self pity was tacked on me by myself, after my love of fifty years and I were in an ugly head-on auto accident. I lost her and got pretty beat up myself. After healing my body and my mind several years, I decided to get with it and think of all the good years we had together and our good trips. She loved to go south to the beach with her sisters and sister-in-law. The Golden Girls. I would go with her when we were younger, but after a few years, I thought how silly to go to the south in the summer, especially when very few of the kin came north. Sometimes, I think it made us closer, being apart for one week a year. Maybe this just justified my adventures and male bonding. Whatever, it's the way it was.

My nephew, Steve, a fly fishing nut also, had just retired from teaching, and was willing to go along. It was a good move, and Steve was a good fishing and camping companion. He put up with my quirks, and we had a good time.

Flying to Calgary, we rented a car and headquartered at Coleman, Alberta, in a motel. Geographically we figured we'd hit every good stream in both Provinces. Yeah, right! Maybe in a couple lifetimes. The good part is we had some great fishing for West Slope cutthroats. We hit some great dry fly hatches, mostly western green drake and caddis. The West Slope cutties are great fighters, although they didn't jump. But tough! Just a chunk of squirming muscle. As much as I hate to use a net, it was necessary to hold them while removing a hook. The country was beautiful but we had the bad luck to have hard rain daily. Even these pristine mountain streams would actually get muddy enough to get us to explore. Seldom would we find a clear stream with good fish.

The other part beside the fishing was the food. We had two great restaurants within a short walk of the motel. The only problem was that you couldn't get small helpings. Even getting a burger on the way there from Calgary airport, they would fill a large dinner plate with a huge burger, fries, pickles, etc. This is just great for some people, and I love to eat, but I just don't hold as much as some people.

We never did get to fish some of the places our friends we got the information from praised, because of rain dirtying them. One stream we kept coming back to was Michel Creek in B.C. It ran parallel for about ten miles or so with paved roads and not too much woodland. Therefore, with easier access, it got fished harder. The beautiful creek fished well, and had good fly hatches regardless. The fish were feisty and willing too. Also, the fish ran from about 12" to about 20" on average. The surprising thing is we seldom caught any smaller ones.

One day while hunting for clear water, we went up the Elk River from Sparwood, B.C. And crossed at a small town by name of Elkwood to a stream called Fording River. It was a pretty stream, and clear, but with a lot of water flowing, same as Elk River. Steve took a side road or trail and dragged bottom a bit with the rental car. He fished down toward where he dropped me off. Once you leave the paved road, it gets wild real quick.

It wasn't too long before I looked upstream and saw Steve coming. The fishing wasn't good there, I guessed, because of the high water. When we met, his face looked a bit pale.

"How come you didn't go farther up river?" I asked.

"The road got too rough and I was afraid of messing up the car. So, I walked up it a bit, and went to the stream. Then, crossing at a shallow riffle, I heard this god-awful thrashing through the trees and brush—coming in my direction. I just froze in the water and thought 'Big Grizzly.' As the noise got very near, I looked up and two big elk came busting into the open and crossed just a few feet in front of me."

"I'm not saying I was scared," said Steve," but if I had a piece of coal between my butt cheeks, it would have turned into a diamond."

We had a good laugh, and I wondered if I would have reacted any differently. Probably not.

While in the general area of Crow's Nest Pass on both Provinces, we saw bear, moose, elk, and two kinds of deer. (No grizzlies.)

Visitors from our home area came to see us at the motel. It was R.B. And Brigette in their motor home. R.B. was a newly retired school teacher like Steve, and Brigette was his new friend. R.B. is an entrepreneur, kind of, with a bicycle shop, horses that he used to rent out at dog trials, wagons and sleighs, and who knows what else.

The day we fished together, we first went to Crow's Nest Creek (named for the pass between Alberta and British Columbia.) We caught some there, mostly small rainbows (different watershed.) Then it was exploring time, to the West Castle River. Why there, I don't know. It is reputed to have North America's highest density of grizzly bears during berry season. This year was a bad crop and most bears went to the other side of the divide to another wild area. Boo Hoo! I didn't see any grizzlies. In reality, the West Castle was a creek which meandered through thick brushy willows of some type. They were so thick that one had a hard time reaching the water. Steve went downstream and me, being the good host, shared pools with R.B. It was a different type of fishing. When we saw a cutthroat cruising, we'd plop a hopper imitation and the fish usually attacked it from a distance. No finesse.

I went ahead of R.B. Briefly, just scouting the next pool. As usual, I was scanning the edge of the water looking for pretty stones, elk teeth, etc. and on the sandy edge with mostly just pieces of twigs with the sand, I saw this stone which stood out like a soda can in this wild, picked it up and it was some sort of artifact shaped like a man. When I got home I asked an archaeologist and he said it's definitely an artifact, but couldn't tell me more. I haven't followed up on it yet.

I no sooner found this than we heard thunder and looked up both sides of the steep, rugged mountains on both sides of the valley, and saw black clouds with lightening flashing around. This was our first sunny day to date and none of us had rain gear in our vests. We beat it toward the road and luckily missed most of the willows and soon made the road. We were already soaked, but made it to the car and waited it out.

Back to the motel where R.B. got permission to park, we got some dry clothes on. Brigette had supper of roast chicken, sweet corn, and some more goodies. She could drive that big motor home and was pretty—a good travel companion for R.B.

Naturally, when Steve and I traveled the four hours back to the Calgary airport, the sun shone the whole way. It was still a good trip and good fishing despite the weather.

I remember when we were at Racehorse Creek, which is up in the mountains, I left Steve along the road while I went to retrieve the car, when I heard this really loud elk bugling. I looked back, expecting it to be near Steve. Later, while we were still up there, at another location, I got back to the car first and was just waiting for my fishing buddy to return. The rich, deep grass around was surrounded by these big beautiful cattle they turn loose up there in the summer to fatten up. I could have opened the car window and petted them.

The next year I was going to stay home, fish, pitch horseshoes, and work on my new home. The other nephew, Bill, ruined these plans with a plan of his own. "Let's go to Colorado and fish the Arkansas River for a short, 4 day trip, if we can get cheap airfare." I'd never fished in Colorado, but he did some checking when he was there with his Dad, and said it would be a lot of dry fly fishing.

The path to Hell is paved with good intentions, and I pay a lot of road tax. We flew to Denver, got a car and drove to Canyon City, got licenses and information. The man at the fly shop said to fish an attractor dry fly with three feet or more dropper with nymphs under it. I thought that could be a nightmare to cast, but only asked about snakes. Fishing this river (the Arkansas) meant hopping the edge among rocks which were everywhere in this canyon land.

"Ahh, just an occasional little one," he said.

Bill got us a small upstairs "motel" at this campground. It was hot as it ever got in that area, and that room they called a motel was *really* hot, even with a fan—no A.C. This place was Cotopax, and was a central location. There were hundreds of rafters floating the river, which surprisingly didn't bother us much. Most of the river was deep and fast in the center, so our fishing was mostly at the edges, and the few wade-able areas. We had a lot of fun with 12" to 14" brown trout. We got no big trout, but lots of action on dry flies, and when we tried the long droppers with nymphs, they worked too, but were hard to cast in the wind.

There was a big-time bicycle race while we were there. They camped everywhere, but I don't remember them pedaling up the miles-long winding road. There were some bad accidents coming down though, and we saw a bad one involving a big truck. We never got a newspaper to find out if any were killed. The road itself wasn't too bad, until you knew how many trucks (logger and dump-type) and buses that were customized to carry rafts and rafters were on it.

Bill and I were fishing just below Salada and were parked at a huge campground. It was all dry with sage brush here and there, and not many campers this far upriver, just a few small pull-behind types and one tent. We walked down a way off the campground and hopscotched each other as we fished up. I got way ahead of Bill and eventually the path ended for me. I went to the top of the steep grade of to the camping area to wait for Bill, rather than go upstream and look for access to the water past the drop-off.

Getting restless, I decided to walk the so-called path through this desert-like campground near the river, to see if I could see Bill coming up the river below me. I caught this movement out of the corner of my eye and glanced over to see a huge rattlesnake (yellow phase) within three feet of me. I somehow hopped on one foot multiple times to get away with my near foot in mid-air. Twenty feet away, I looked back and saw what I thought was a six-foot or more rattler as big around as my arm, slithering down the bank toward a big juniper or pine to hide. I tried to warn the people in the nearby tent, but no one was there at the time. I wish the owner of the fly shop at Canyon City would see that one up close sometime!

The rattlesnake, that most people thought I was too excited and scared to identify, was in its yellow phase, as opposed to some in Pennsylvania, that get a black phase also.

More dangerous than snakes were the steep banks to the river. Bill and I both used wading staffs even when the water didn't seem treacherous.

Sometimes the paths were just loose rocks that would roll all or most of the way down when bumped. The wading staffs, if we didn't hit solid rock, would dig in enough so we didn't take any nasty spills.

One particular spot was especially treacherous, and after reaching the river and fishing, I noticed, finally, that the rougher it was to reach the water, the better the fishing. Makes sense. I got behind Bill and he was fishing toward a cliff that I knew we couldn't get around. I looked back to the place we'd come down, and decided I'd climb this semi-cliff where I had ledges to hold onto. It was slow, and hot, and I knew if I started sliding there'd be hell to pay. I made it OK, sweating, and got rehydrated again.

Bill ran into muddy water, due to a small mountain stream that got a hard rain, about the same place upstream where he couldn't wade any farther, so he retreated and found a way up. He was beat when he got up there and hadn't brought his water with him. Although Bill is in good shape for his age (he was nearing 60 at the time) he was getting light-headed and shaky. He rehydrated, and realized the importance of keeping water with him at all times when it's hot. He still thinks he's young and bullet-proof, and still plays ice hockey several times a week. He doesn't listen to his old sage uncle's good advice, even yet. Of course, I was already over 70 when I flirted with death by climbing that cliff.

Bill was ready to quit for the day, because he was still a bit shaky. Salada was only a few miles on up, and we stopped at a nice restaurant and had a nice meal, and plenty of iced tea. Bill liked the food there, as most restaurants had hot and spicy Tex-Mex food. After we ate, we drove up to the exit of Black's Canyon, where we fished just half-heartedly, and enjoyed the scenery and rafters coming down. For a four day trip, we had good fishing, saw some new rocks, different type fishing, and beautiful, rugged scenery.

We took a side trip to a tourist-type canyon (can't remember its name.) It was a huge deep pit in the Earth with a small swinging bridge across it. At one time I was an ironworker and climbed steel, but no way would I get on that bridge. Crazier yet, on the other side opposite us, were these telephone poles rigged with a slide-like thing with a swing for nutty daredevils. It would come to the end and these people, one at a time, would swing out over the canyon, which was hundreds of feet high. It made me squeamish just to see them.

Our second trip by air out to British Columbia we flew to Kalispell, Montana, and drove to Fernie, B.C. in a rental. One of our guys rented a ski lodge which was cheaper and nicer than the motel that Steve and I had used previously. Good restaurants were not as close as at Coleman, Alberta. Our gang this trip was nephew Bill, Walt H., Jon, and I. We decided we couldn't fish all the streams in B.C. let alone Alberta. We had two rental cars, as Bill had to be back sooner than the rest of us, this worked out well, especially for fishing smaller streams, where we could spread out better. Walt had three float trips on the Elk River set up: Bill and him on one, Walt with me on one, and Jon and I on another. It was a new experience for several of us. The outfitter had a fit when he insisted the guides recommend dry flies only. Dry flies are more fun and more visible, but after only a few fish, we told the guide we would give them something they'd eat. Sculpin imitations were presented and the west slope cutties thought they were manna from cuttie heaven. We just tore them up. Several bull trout were caught too. The outfitter only found out when another guide heard about it when we got back. The amount of money he charged us, plus a generous tip to the guide, I don't see how the owner could appoint the river a dry fly only fishery. We used all artificials, pinched the barbs shut, and returned all fish unharmed.

I felt bad for our guide, but the guys wouldn't let me give the man in charge my opinion of his arrogant rules for them.

One morning Bill, who was on the ground floor of the lodge with me, called me to the window in his room to show me a moose in the woods. There had been a small black bear below our area earlier. On a trip to Michele Creek, I saw mule deer, white tail deer, and a small elk. No grizzlies, and that's all right with me.

The day I fished with Jon, we took a long trip to the Wigwam River. We got some there, but access to other parts were rough getting to, and the downstream part was blocked by thick woods and steep banks, so after catching several, I decided to fish up a small feeder stream to the road, then see if Jon was up near where we started. A deep hole as small as my bathroom, at a bend in the stream, ran into a downed evergreen tree.

"I'll bet there's a cutthroat in there, if I can get him out without catching a branch."

Sure enough, on the first drift with a stone nymph, I felt "tap-tap-tap" and set the hook on a really nice cutty which I had to "horse in" to keep it away from the branches. It ended up being my biggest of the trip, in the smallest stream that I fished. (I'm not saying it was big, but the picture of it weighed four pounds.) Actually, it was 20-22" but we caught many 15-18" fish.

I met up with Jon and he was ready to go back and try more small streams. The next bridge we came to, we pulled off, had a snack, and I went up and Jon went down. I don't know what was in the water, but that was the slipperiest stream I ever waded. I didn't do well up so I came back down where I started, and Jon was into a nice one. I got a picture of him and after he lost it, I asked, "How big?" Naturally, after it was gone, he gave an exaggerated arm spread. It turned out he'd found a big hole under the bridge, and a good hatch was on. He caught several while I struggled upstream. I didn't see the hatch at first in the broken water. Finally I went below to the bridge hole and caught several.

It was a great day, even though Jon had a much better day catching fish than I did. We went back to the lodge, hung up the waders and cleaned some of the stink off us, and went out and had a great supper. The funny thing is, I'm more of a meat-and-potatoes person, but when in Canada, I make it a point to order Caesar salad. So far, no matter where in Canada, it's great there. I've heard it has something to do with using raw eggs, and they're not allowed to do that in the U.S.

Bill left early, and it had been a good trip, but long, and I was beat. I suggested to the other guys that they fish together the next day, and I would stay back and rest. I tried to convince them that I wasn't sick or mad at anything, just tired and happy. I'm not sure they believed me, but it was true, that I can turn my back on great fishing when I'm sated. I've done it before. I just don't need to lick the wrapper.

They decided they had enough too (I hope not for my sake) and we left the next day to visit Glacier National Park. So, we got back through the border into Montana and did the tourist trip. We got a bite to eat and some ice cream, and browsed through the souvenirs. Not my idea of fun, except the eats.

Finally we got to the park and did the motor tour. There were lots of tourists and lots of scenic country. I was impressed with MacDonald Lake. It had a milky tint and all the stones along the shores were oval and smooth. There wasn't much left of the glaciers and we had trouble seeing what was left, because of smoke from a forest fire, some miles away. It covered a whole section of the state. We even saw a black bear across a stream that paralleled the road. Eventually, we got on the "Sun Road" which I thought was really neat, but scary, because of the thousand foot drop-offs from the edge of the narrow, cliff-hanging road. These old reconditioned tourist cars were there, and I had to wonder if any, with their original brakes and tires, ever went over the side.

Eventually we turned our rental car (van) in and caught the plane home. I only had a week to wash my clothes, pay my bills, repack my clothes and pills, go to the bank, and mow the grass, before I could head to Labrador with another crew, to try for big brook trout and see how the rich people lived. I told my kids I was spending all their inheritance, and it wasn't far off the truth.

CHAPTER TEN—LABRADOR

I like to *be* places, but I hate the hassle to get there. This trip involved a trip from Central PA to Annapolis, MD, then an overnight stay at Dave's house. The next day we picked up Bill (yes, another Bill) and headed for the airport.

Dave was originally from our area, and has a veterinary clinic in the Annapolis area. Walt is a local that I often fish with, and Bill lives in Dave's area. He's a semi-retired, jolly landscaper that once did the Pentagon lawns. At least, that's how we introduced him to everyone.

Checking through customs at Montreal was fun as usual, and so was the hikes through airports, especially for Bill's gimpy legs. Bill loves to gamble, so we stayed overnight (this was planned ahead) and went to a casino. After donating to the French-Canadians, we went to our rooms. We headed to Labrador the next day.

To the best of my knowledge, there are only two towns in Labrador, across the water from each other. The only paved roads are there also. Labrador and Newfoundland are the same province. Newfoundland is a large island just off the mainland and has a much larger population. At the lodge, the help, camp, kitchen, and guides, are all "Newfies," which I'm told is primarily Irish immigrants. They're a tough, hardy, and friendly group of people. I was starting to worry when, near the end of the week, I was beginning to understand their fast-talking brand of English, not so much like the Irish of Eire, but their own brand of accent.

Anyhow, the next morning, we flew to the lodge in a "Beaver," the tough, powerful plane of the North. From the air, the terrain looks like there are equal parts water and land, which explains why there are not many people there year-round. Another reason is the weather, as it's nasty in the winter, which starts in September or October there.

There are other roads, all dirt, that we saw from the air, which mainly connected mining operations. There was one large lake that was completely discolored to a red color due to mining. I don't think lumbering, or logging, amounted to much there, unless it was for paperwood, because the trees were small, scrubby things.

Animal life included caribou, black bear, porcupine, a few beaver, which the one young guide hated because they spread giardia.) The caribou had just moved their routes from our area recently. They feed on lichens, moss-like plants which take a decade or more to mature. The caribou move on when their grazing thins the lichens out. Caribou are the main critters of the latitude where we were, but I saw none. A glimpse of a beaver is the only land animal I saw on that trip. Of fish, there were brook trout, lake trout, and northern pike, though Dave got a whitefish or rough fish of some type on a fly. There were suckers also. Later, arctic char arrived from salt water to spawn.

Finally, the next morning, we took off and landed back at the lodge (float planes of course) and we were greeted by the entire staff of the Newfies. They helped us to the different cabins, which were quite nice, considering where we were. A big generator powered the whole place. I have no idea how they got the big stuff there. Maybe some sort of boat route or possibly a snowmobile train. A portable sawmill had been set up to do much of the heavier cutting, and I suspect a planer was used too, as opposed to flying in all finished wood. An "Otter" was available too, to fly larger loads. It's also a de Havilland like the Beaver, only larger.

We had a quick meal and were taken out to fish, one guide to two clients. We were motored in a 20-22' canoe across the lake to where a stream came in. Dave and Bill stayed at the mouth, and "Sandy" Mullin took Walt and me up a bunch of caribou trails, about a mile of rough walking where the stream was faster over broken water. Walt was a bit overwhelmed by the thick brush right up to the water, as I was. I was above him, and got on top of a big boulder. I cast an olive woolie bugger across this deep, swirly hole and felt a solid strike part-way back.

This is easy, I thought, as I worked the 17" brookie back to me. I was fired up! Cranked! Several casts later, I got another almost as big. End of the easy fishing! From then on we fished the area, trying to find room to cast, and find nicer holes. More fish were caught, but they were all smaller. We couldn't find any surface (dry fly) fishing.

Several hours later, it was time to go back, as we had a long walk and a long boat ride ahead. Walt stepped in a soggy hole and fell, breaking his fly rod. The other two fished out of the boat, as Bill couldn't handle the walking. Dave was (is) in great shape and would get out of the boat and fish wherever possible. Dave gets bored easily and loves to explore and walk, even if it's just around a river or lake shoreline. At home, he's a good turkey hunter, though sometimes I wonder how he can be still long enough to be successful. He had a pile of fly boxes and was always changing flies. Walt nick-named him "Gas-Ass" because he's always traveling somewhere. He must have a great crew at his vet clinic, that he can be on the go so much. His wife is a lawyer, and she's always on the go also.

Bill and I fished together one day from the large canoes, using basic spin outfits, with a different Newfie guide. He went along another day also, to "Rick's Surprise," a cigar-shaped lake with a small stream that also had brook trout in it. A famous Celtics basketball player, Bill Havlicek, caught an 8 lb. brookie there, according to lodge owner Robin Reeve, from Vermont. Dave and I went to "Cigar Lake," another name for Rick's Surprise. Rick was Robin's brother, and this was his farewell trip, as he passed away the next winter. The brothers were just exploring and flying from spot to spot. This little lake is basically land-locked—therefore the surprise that brook trout were there.

Dave and I caught some brookies—none over 15" in the tiny stream going into the lake. We were up there the last week of their season, and most of the large brookies were done with the streams and back to the lakes. One trip there was a bonus fly-out as they just wanted to repair an old fiberglass boat they had stashed there, that a bear had chewed up. The first-year guide was strong and willing, but didn't know much about fishing, at least for trout. He took Dave and me in the boat with one oar missing. The small lake was loaded with northern pike, and after we got several, we quit, because it was just too hard to maneuver the boat with one oar. The day Bill and I trolled for lake trout we got several, plus a few pike on the big lake where the main camp was. They were big, strong, healthy fish, and it was a novelty for me, just not my cup of tea.

The one bigger river they took us to, we actually could see several huge brookies about five to eight pounds, or larger. Try as we could, we just couldn't fool them. At one time, there were two males and one female only a few feet from me. I tried lots of different flies with no success. I always figured that if I could see them, they could see me, unless they were upstream facing the current. I knew from reading John Gierach's *Another Lousy Day in Paradise* that even if we were there at a prime time, which we weren't, it would be tough to catch them. We were there the last week before they closed up the camp for the year. If I haven't learned anything else over the years, I've learned to take what the defense gives you, and if it's a good defense, try to enjoy your day anyhow.

While being flustered, I saw Walt and Quentin, the Newfie guide of the day, waving, pointing and peering in the water. Walt's rod wasn't bowed, so I knew there was no fish on. Later I walked down and asked what they were so excited about. Walt told about this eight pound brookie that looked like it was swimming sideways. As it headed out of the current into the side eddy, and the glare lessened, they realized a huge pike had the trout in its mouth! If you didn't realize before why there weren't more big brookies up there, this helped explain it. Once they get out of the small, fast feeder streams and into pike-infested waters, only the wariest and luckiest trout (char, actually) survive until adulthood. Then there's the rough weather in the sub-arctic region to consider.

After a cup of coffee with Walt, (Quentin had tea, as most Newfies preferred,) I walked back to where I'd been before and continued to fish. Mid-afternoon, I got bored with no trout, and cast into an eddy with a black woolie bugger and immediately had a hard strike that cleaned my fly off the leader. Pike, I thought, then tied on another one, then the same result. "You dummy," I said to myself. This time I put on a knottable wire leader. After satisfying my lust for a few big pike (11 or 12 actually) I let Marco, our French Canadian pilot, catch a couple. He was retiring after this week. What a character! This wildman was relatively young yet. I don't think he was quitting altogether, just this area, then going back to Quebec where he lived.

His replacement, another French Canadian naturally, was kind of over dressed, style-wise, for the wilderness. I was lucky enough to be on board for his first landing on a small wild lake. The afore-mentioned Cigar Lake was the target. He made a pass-over to see where the sandbar was and to make sure there weren't any logs, trees, or rocks, then went back and nicely put it down on the edge away from the sandbar. Apparently he flew before in other parts of Canada.

Depending on how late it was after another great supper, we'd play a "Texas hold 'em" game, or cribbage (a Newfie favorite and also mine.) Our favorite guide, Sandy, I believe won both hold 'em games, and I was second. The last night there, Robin, the owner, was sucking down wine pretty good, and he was also very competitive. Anyhow, I was partnered with Francis, the cook. She was considered the best at cribbage. Because I was an unknown factor, I was allowed to play. I'd played this for years and did OK. Robin and his partner were way ahead of us and only needed 1 or 2 to "peg out" and win. They even got to count first. Francis and I were 20 or 21 behind. We both stacked low cards (our only chance) for pegging. If you ever played or knew anything about cribbage, you'd know we had a mountain to climb. We did the impossible and pegged out and won, and Robin and his partner were stunned. Well, he bad-mouthed Francis with some foul language, and I just glared at him and hoped he got the message. He might have been rich through good business sense, and built a classy set-up in the wilds of Labrador, but he had no class as a person. The cook and her husband, Kevin, who was camp manager, and her sister, who helped her in the kitchen, were his employees and kept their mouths shut. But, I think my glaring at him finally shut him up.

The outpost camp was the last full day of fishing. After flying there and stowing our personals, we got into our waders and fishing gear. It was the four of us, and Walt and I had Sandy, and Bill and Dave had Quentin. Quentin was a tall, husky kid, a bit self-important and immature. The guides were both brutes. They'd get out of those big canoes at some of the rapids and tow us upstream, and later, downstream, led us through the potentially dangerous rocks.

Finally, Walt, Sandy and I stopped at rapids or riffles between lakes. The others headed out of sight, up another set of rapids. Sandy put us both in a spot and scanned the water for trout, but didn't find any. The guides' young eyes are trained to pick out the brightly colored male brookies. Resigned, I cast weighted sculpin imitations and nymphs to the swifter, deeper side, to no avail. After an hour or more, I did a 180* and waded about fifty feet to a bit more gentle stretch. I liked this better for dry flies and put on a #14 bluewing olive of my own design (extended body.) Since no trout were in sight, I just concentrated on getting a good natural drift, and to possible targets where a trout might lie. I'd cast awhile to my near side, then to a long drift toward the main run. I was getting pretty good drifts and casts, as it wasn't too windy. Daydreaming, but still trying with my fly, it drifted past my main near target and a big slurp appeared tight to the rock. Sandy was there, noticed, and said, "Strike! Strike!"

Amazingly, I was already calmly setting the hook, and after a few strong runs, realized it was a big, golden-bellied male. This is what the trip was about. I was able to keep him out of the heavy run into the deep pool below, where I was afraid of him being eaten by a big pike or lake trout. Having just returned from B.C. and big trout there, I was ahead of Sandy's directions for fighting it. We got some pictures and took it up in the net to show Walt, then released him. It wasn't a giant, but probably five pounds, and beautiful. Later I got another maybe four to four-and-a-half pound female off the edge of the other run, not nearly as pretty (except to me.) Then again, females aren't usually as colorful as males in the fish and animal world, just in the human world. The other guys weren't as successful as I was, and I felt bad for them.

The weather turned crappy, and we had a two hour motor canoe ride through pouring cold rain and wind. Fortunately, we all had good rain gear. After getting back into warm, dry clothes, (yes, some rain got to us,) Sandy finished getting a spaghetti meal ready, and Quentin went out with the one canoe. He soon came back with a nice lake trout, then they cleaned it and baked it. We all had a great meal and a friendly hold 'em game, which Sandy won. He and I dueled for an hour after the others sacked out.

The plane picked us up the next day after we trolled the area awhile for lake trout. Then to the main lodge for another good evening meal, and to pack to go home. We were picked up by a big Otter and it hauled all the guests back to the civilized world.

CHAPTER ELEVEN—
GREEN DRAKE TIME

The green drake hatch, or emergence, is probably the best known, or at least, most popular in the Eastern USA. I've counted license plates from many states in the different parking lots. It gets to be somewhat of a circus at times. I've seen and counted 18 cars in a private parking lot on Penn's which should only hold 8 at the most. The stream itself is much more crowded than opening week. Even at ten o'clock at night, I've seen drunks falling in the water, rolling down steep hills, and just being rude in general.

The size flies that bring the larger fish to the surface are huge compared to the #14 to #20 that one would normally use. A size #8 tied on a #10 hook is about right. Some people tie them as big as birds and proceed to catch fish on them. One day I was on lower Broadwater scanning the water for rises, when I looked several hundred yards upstream on the white mountain side and saw a shad fly (that's what locals call them) that dwarfed the others. Shocked and amazed, I watched as it slowly flew in my direction. The big, beautiful, cream and greenish bug got nearer and then I realized it wasn't a miracle—it was a big Luna moth that resembled the green drake in color but not in size.

The evening I was just below the special regulation water when there were, I guess, about sixty fishermen downstream that we could see. There may have been more, that were back away from the water, waiting for the magic moment when the spinners come over the stream from the trees to mix in with the males which were dancing up and down the edge of the trees. Then the "swarm" comes when the air is full of these mayflies. If you're in the current, they get down your neck, under your glasses, up your sleeve, inside your shirt—the air is cream colored even after dark, when it usually occurs.

This evening I decided to stay up the creek where there weren't quite as many people. As it turned out, I missed all the excitement, as a good-sized bear decided to cross Penn's right in the midst of the crowd, just before dark. A friend of mine who was downstream wasn't bear-shy unless he was directly threatened. He said within five minutes after the bear crossed, he could have fished anywhere he wanted to.

Late one night there was a good swarm and I was stationed at the tail of Broadwater under some trees and it was shallow there. I had fair fishing there as lots of drowned drakes were funneled near me where it flared into riffles below me. I began to hear a lot of loud cursing and yelling up-current from me. Someone's having a bad day, I thought. It kept up with louder, different voices, and now closer to me. Soon, an aluminum canoe was headed my way.

"Stay over towards the middle a bit as it's really low where I am," I said as he was already ricocheting off rocks, and making a lot of noise. He had to get out of the canoe—he was alone—and since I wasn't threatening, he decided to take a chance to talk.

"What in hell kind of mess did I get into?" he whined. "People cursed me, threw rocks at me, and shone flashlights in my eyes, blinding me. There are people everywhere! What are they all doing in the middle of the woods this time of night? And how far is it to Weikert?"

I chuckled a bit, amused by his distress.

"Pal, you should have done your homework," I said, explaining a bit about the "tourist hatch" as I call it. "If you want to pull your canoe out here, it would be as good a place as any until morning. I'll help you. It's a good five miles, depending on where you take out. Also, even though you won't run into as many fishermen, you have a lot of low riffles and rocks, and you have no flashlight."

"Oh crap," he said, "I just have to get back tonight."

"Well," I said, "Good luck! And don't get in such a hurry that you get hurt."

My fishing was done for the night, but thinking about the canoer, I had a much better night than he'd have. I'll bet he never explores again without a bit of planning.

Twice I took people along just so they could see the phenomenon of the green drake swarm. The first one was Don, a fellow Postal employee. He was no fly rodder, so he didn't fish. He was game to go along though, and we only went part way to Broadwater. Due to all the people, I kind of got wedged in to a tricky place to fish. Although a nice fish-holding spot, it was tough to get a natural drift. I ended up going to the end of the spot where it was swift and belt-deep. It worked out well, as I had to cast upstream and the fly drifted true back to me. Also I could get some glare from the sky and see OK. I sat on the rocks at the edge talking to Don, while he smoked one cigarette after another. The swarm came, and he'd never seen anything like it. Then the first fish started feeding in an easy spot. I eased out in the current and after several casts, I hooked and landed a nice 14" brown. I eased over and showed it to Don. Then another trout came up in the same place. There was a repeat performance. Again Don was impressed. Before I got done fluffing out my hair wing fly, another fish came up in the same spot. Same results. It was getting uncanny. I must have caught 10 or 11 fish and all but 2 or 3 from the exact same spot. They were all nice fish within an inch of the same size. No real big ones, no small ones. A great evening any way I looked at it. I explained to Don it was a much better night than usual. He fishes bass and has done Canadian trips with me, and he understood. A bad day fishing is better than a good day at work.

Gary was the other person I showed the swarm to, and he was also impressed. The fishing wasn't as good as usual, but he was trying with an outfit I rigged for him. Soon I got involved with fishing, trying to find a good spot. Gary went on his own and we got separated. I didn't know if he had a flashlight or not, but I recommended he not use it unless he had to change flies or follow the path back, because he would lose his night vision, which was true.

Later, he found me at the parking lot with the fly deeply embedded in his thumb. Apparently he was reeling his line in to quit with the leader between his thumb and finger. He didn't realize it was close and zap! Into his thumb. I wanted to back it out because "It took me a half an hour to tie that fly" as I blend the different colored hair before tying the fly. I lost the argument and also a perfectly good fly. He still "ouched" and said bad words, but wouldn't let me back the fly out even though I had pinched the barb almost shut. Eventually we cut the fly off at the bend of the hook.

As you've gathered, every trip is not productive. Why is it that we always hear about the good days and nights? One word, and this includes me: EGO! But I do have bad days, and plenty of them. Like forgetting my rod. Or falling in, or losing fly boxes or rods by not stowing them properly. Like leaving them on my truck cap roof and later driving over my rod when I realized it was left on the roof.

I usually remember the days when they were only partly bad, then God realizes you've been punished enough and pulls a certain switch, and life is good again. Like one day I got to a favorite spot and it was yellow muddy, and it hadn't rained 25 miles away at home. I had time to fish, and I was rigged with green drake, so I went to the stream and thought that I had things I should be doing at home. Regardless, I began to cast close to rocks and drifting a fly through shallows. After a while a fish rose, then gulped my shad fly. That was odd, I thought. While I fluffed my fly, another fish rose. Then another—and more. Then there was a full fledged emergence of green drakes on and it was daylight. The fish were easier because of the dirty water, and no one else was fishing. I felt kind of guilty because I had no one to share it with. Then in the middle of it, I was upstream and I heard this wild yelling. Thinking it was one of my boys with an emergency at home, I hustled down the treacherous walking and wading to find out it was an old pal's son. He was basically a super kid, married and with a kid, but he had a bad problem with drugs and booze. He was out in his own world at the time, so I said, "Jim, I'm into really good fishing right now, and I'm going back and enjoy it. Please get in your car and sleep it off, rather than drive home." He appeared to settle down a bit, but the fishing and the hatch, and my zeal, all went downhill. I still had a good day fish-wise. Jim was a local policeman and called me soon after the episode. He apologized sincerely and said he'd been fighting this for a long while, and thought he almost had it whipped. Several months later I read in the paper that he overdosed and died. It didn't surprise me too much as it happens all the time, locally, and in the news. God must have pulled the switch and said, "Jim, you deserve some peace."

The owner of the camp where I usually park on Penn's Creek has four boys. So do I, plus a girl which is my oldest. Several of our boys ran together when they were younger, as we lived in the same neighborhood. Naturally, as their camp was next to the creek, his boys like to fish. (At least the green drake hatch.) They sweet-talked me into giving them some of my flies because they knew they caught fish. I thought they would last them the season, as to cast them without the big flies spinning and twisting, a heavy leader (tippet) should be used. I didn't get over to the stream until late on the drake hatch. The two boys saw me park my vehicle and were immediately trying to bum more of my "special" flies.

"What happened to the ones I gave you?" I asked.
"The big ones broke our flies off," they said. "They were really big fish!"
"How big? Did you see them?"
"No, they broke off when we set the hook," said Alex.
"What size leader was on the rod?" I questioned.
"The same as we used for the sulfurs," they answered.
That explained it, as either I or their dad probably rigged them with a 5x tippet for sulfurs. They probably also got excited and drove the hook home with authority. Maybe lost some on the back-cast or on overhead branches.

Anyhow, I gave them each one more, and explained to them to use heavier tippet and make them last, because I didn't have time to tie more. When I did tie, I used a much simpler pattern, and still do. I don't think it makes much difference, except in my own mind. Throughout the years I've seen scores of different pattern and each owner swears theirs is the most effective a person could use. Many didn't resemble the natural at all except most of the better ones were the right size and had lots of hair and feathers. Remember, this was mostly night fishing and when they looked up they didn't see colors or a perfect form. Each fly, when they did their reproductive act, fell dead or dying on the water in all different ways. If there's any strategy, it's to get the timing and rhythm of a trout feeding and try to pass your bug over the fish at that time without drag. Tie some hair and dog poo on a hook and if you you find a fish feeding good, he'll take it.

The most successful fishermen for "the tourist hatch" are the ones that can locate fish that are feeding with regularity, and present a natural drift.

Even the novices and part-time fly fishers will get some, because during and after the swarm there are thousands and thousands of spent bugs all over the water. Many of the old timers, and others that drag their feet about using a fly, will pick the naturals out of the trees and fish a "bouquet" where allowed. They catch fish too, but . . .

Sometimes, the early morning after a good swarm, it can be exciting just prospecting pocket water with a big dry green drake. I was doing this one morning way down the creek and had fun catching and also drawing trout out that didn't get the fly. I came to a long pool called Aumiller's Flat. I would locate a feeding fish and hooked some, but most would rise, examine my fly, then refuse it. A gentleman I've met on the stream often, from the D.C. Area, followed behind me and caught most that had refused my fly.

"What are you using?" I asked when we both took a break to tell lies. He showed me a big, all-white deer-hair fly, and that stunned me—not that he out-fished me, which has often happened, but that it was a bright sunny day and he was using an all white fly and fishing behind me. Very humbling! I have tied white flies (not as nice as his) since, and caught some fish on them, but not with regularity like he did.

Fishing upstream near Love's Hole one sunny day with little success, a fellow came out of the woods, where he was by-passing me, even though I was just looking at the water for rises.

"I just wanted to thank you!" he burst out.

"What for? I don't believe I even know you."

"Oh yeah, you're the same guy. A few years back, I was on Penn's for the first time, fishing the drakes very unsuccessfully, and you gave me one of your flies. Look! I still have it."

Sure enough, it was one of my old blended hair wing flies. Even after a nice streamside chat, I still didn't remember him, and I wasn't even senile then.

Early on, before the emergence gets a full head of steam, I was fishing green drake nymphs in some nice pocket water just above the special regulation area. After some success, maybe three fish, I noticed two attractive young women fishing nymphs on the other side. One said, "What are you using?" I told her, and she waded over the shallow riffles, wanting to see my pattern. It was the same as the shops tie in State College.

"That's not like mine," she said. "We took a class from Joe Humphries." That explained why they were fishing the more shallow pockets like Spring Creek has.

She showed me hers, and I showed her mine. (No pun intended.)

Her pattern looked to me like my stone nymph pattern, so I showed my stone nymph.

"Yes, that looks like Joe's drake nymph," she said, not convinced.

"Your fly (nymph) is a good choice because the stone flies are active now also." But since she still wasn't sure, I waded to a dead pocket in the weeds at the shoreline and grabbed a handful of spent nymph shucks from the night before. I explained what they were. Then I picked a dry stone nymph shuck from a rock and showed her the difference.

"I'm sure you just got them mixed up," I said, "but now that you've seen the real thing you'll know. Oh, and fish more of the larger pockets on Penn's, you'll do better."

She thanked me and said, "We'll know next time." For now, they had to go home and pick up their kids at the school bus stop.

Bob, a tough little (smaller than me) fellow, fished Penn's occasionally, usually wet flies. He never seemed to want to experiment with matching the hatch. He was a very intense guy that fished with his upper body bent forward, and usually had a chew in his mouth. The green drakes would come and he would fish every night, following the hatch from Weikert as it advanced all the way to Coburn. He fished bouquets (live) and usually fished late, like 2 or 3 o'clock in the morning, then open his gas station at 6AM each day. He caught lots of really nice fish, but had to have suffered physically. In some years of steady cooler weather, it would take the hatch as long as two weeks to complete its circuit for the year. I like to catch big fish too, but never considered myself to be a trophy hunter. I just like to catch fish and be out there. Bob was not a bragging type that took pictures or even showed off his catch. I could never understand that mentality, but they're out there. Obsessed, I guess, is the word.

Years back, maybe in the 1950's, when I just began to fish Penn's Creek, I would get my live green drakes to fish bouquets from a local stream. Honey Creek has a hatch, but not in the numbers you need to pick them for bait. Another stream, the west branch of Kishacoquillas Creek, was loaded with them, but the stream was not noted for its fishing. Before I began to fish flies, progress killed all the fly life on the pretty stream. An ammonia spill from a dairy or ice cream plant at Belleville was responsible and was never properly punished for it. Sixty years later, it is still trying to recover, even with several class A streams feeding life into it. Oh, what could have been, if that stream had stayed healthy.

Big Walt and I got started late one evening. Actually, we didn't feel like trying to "nail down" a hot spot. Other people would be fishing nearby all evening anyway. So we spent extra time talking at the parking lot with Bill, the camp owner, and eventually loaded up with water and cigars (for the bugs.)

"This should be a three-cigar night, Walt," I guessed.

"Yeah, I hope so, if we can find a spot to fish," he replied.

Everywhere we went there were gobs of fisherpersons. Finally, we went back upstream and found a short stretch of fast water that was deep enough to hold some good fish. Trouble was that after dark in the riffley water, it would be hard to follow the fly and locate the fish. So we fired up cigar number one and began the wait. (I finally quit cigars a few years ago.) Walt was just above me and I was near two big rocks, so I could sit while waiting. I didn't tell Walt that.

Eventually the swarm started early enough to see fairly well. We each caught several right away. I had to back off the rock I was on in order to cast tight to the boulder where several trout were feeding. Walt ran out of fish soon, but I was still locating feeders, some just by sound. I even lucked into one I couldn't see, but hooked when I heard the "gulp' where my fly should have been.

It was wild for a while and we felt lucky to do as well as we did. Meanwhile, we weren't too far from the car, but the fog moved in and was quite thick. Both of us with flashlights tried to find the path as we went up the grade toward it. "Damn, how did we miss it?" I whined as we were getting into thicker and thicker brush. Finally, we saw a dim glow through the pea soup fog that had to be the camp. They usually lit a Coleman lantern. We plowed through the brush and came to the lot—never did find the path, which was an old logging road about ten feet wide. We both must have crossed over it and missed it in the fog.

I have even guided a group of strangers up the path from Broadwater, almost a mile away, when none of us had a flashlight. Amazed, one fellow asked me how I could do it.

"Easy," I explained, "When you start walking through leaves and brush, you're off the path."

The green drake hatch (tourist hatch) is about over, and things will get back to normal soon. A person will be able to park at his favorite spot, fish some days and see no or few fly fishers, see tubers as the weather warms more. The parking lot stories will lessen as the crowd dwindles (this is the part I'll miss.) The blue wing olives will be starting soon and you can fish them before it's too dark. Isonychias will be appearing, some cahills, potomatnas, if you like to fish after dark, and more "no fish no action" days.

But, wait a minute! Is it really over? Some people, myself included, don't like to follow the bugs upstream. I prefer to fish the same few miles for the whole process, to watch the stages as they come and go. I like to go out when most fishermen and most of the bugs are gone. The trout that aren't gorged with food remember those big bugs and some late bloomers are still around. I've been skunked most of these times, but I've had some evenings when, if I was patient, listened for gulps, and fished some good water where I could locate some. I'd still get a few fish with good memories. I have a nephew that's more hard-headed than me that would go out even after I gave up, and had good fishing.

Eventually, it's really over, and you can have lots of fun with other types of fishing. But there's nothing like shad flies to bring up big fish with regularity.

CHAPTER TWELVE— THE PARKING LOT

The parking lot is where all the fishermen gather to put on their gear and tell their exaggeratd stories. It can be where the boats are put in or a state park or just a pull-off along a dirt road. I don't think most fishermen lie. I know some exaggerate quite a bit, but I don't think the lie. Exception! Some lie to pad their egos. I think most are like me and tell it the way we remember things. I've been accused of underestimating by some people, but not often. Do I lie when I play Texas Hold 'em? You bet! But that's another game.

Actually, the truth makes a better story. For instance, one day I came back to my vehicle (yes, in the parking lot) for a break at Penn's Creek. Another vehicle, a pick-up, was blocking the lane just past the camp and two fellows were sitting on the tailgate, peeling corn off cobs and tossing it out on the ground. I watched them warily, and one of them caught my eye and pointed over the bank. I eased up and peeked, and there was a full-grown peacock. What in hell was a peacock doing on the mountain, twenty miles from the nearest farm? I never found the answer to that, but it turned out they were trying to chum it close enough to dive out and catch it. They said they almost got it once. Did you ever see the spurs on one of them? As big as they are, they could hurt you just by flogging a person.

Anyhow, the bird wandered away through the brush and I never saw it again or heard of it. I often wondered if a coyote or fox eventually got it. I know those guys didn't, and should be glad they didn't catch it. It would have been fun to watch though.

A fellow that fished Penn's (I'll call him Smitty) was a worm fisherman, and very good at it. He often fished with another hefty guy. They weren't fat, just husky. Each had these long rods, 12', I believe. They'd reach out and get perfect drifts through each small pocket in the broken water and do a job on the trout. They fished the "open" water and killed some, but not many fish. One day on the stream, I met a woman with a 12' rod and she was catching fish too. Later, I saw her at the parking area and we talked fishing awhile, when Smitty drove in, and guess who taught her the long rod technique?

Different times, Joe Humphries and I were both there when Smitty was there, and we'd both try as hard as we could to convert him to flies, but he'd refuse. We both knew, even though he had a unique technique, he put the bait to the right places without drag. We even offered him flies to get started with. It would have simplified his fishing, no bait to fool with, but I think he was afraid we were right.

Lots of my fishing buddies loved to go to Potter County. I never cared for it much, I guess because I never seemed to find much in the way of hatches. Also, it seemed to have mostly fish that were native—to hatcheries. I believe most people remember the old stocking formula: load up kettle Creek and others to bring tourist dollars into that underpopulated county. At that time, we used a lot of salmon eggs, and the freshly stocked rainbows loved them. Now, some of us, me included, still use eggs, but now they're artificial flies, blow bugs.

Well, Tom and Stan and I went up for a few days. After work, I worked—they were teachers. I don't know how I got mixed up with so many teachers. We got there late and set up a tent and were starved.
There were few eating places around, so we decided on bacon and eggs as they were faster and easier. Tom was still unmarried at that time, and Stan was not an accomplished camper. I was getting out the gear while they held flashlight. I cooked some bacon first (they forgot cooking oil.) As they got out paper plates (no silverware) I searched for a spatula. None! So, we had scrambled eggs made with a huge BBQ fork. Oh yeah! Tom and I had coffee, which filled us up. We made a list in case we could find a store: can opener (for the Dinty Moore stew,) plastic tableware, etc.

In those days, Tom liked to fish alone in long, remote stretches, so Stan and I dropped him off along the road, and picked him up hours later, after we did some fish searching ourselves. Ol' Tom knows how to survive, by drinking a huge Stoney's beer one of the Jones brothers gave him. The Jones boys were a neat pair. They live in different parts of the state now. They had a good supply of Stoneys, a small brewery in the northern part of PA. They wanted to show us their secret camping spot, with a small stream running near it. After getting directions, we went back to eat and get the fishing gear off.

Eventually we went up this small, rocky Jeep trail and saw some gas wells along the way. Finally we got to the camp, and the brothers were drinking Stoneys and Tom and Stan had one also. (I don't drink beer, although later, I began to make fruit brandy.) Tom and I made our way up the grade to examine a gas well which was about 75 feet away from a big bonfire they had going. As we were looking the well over, Tom began sniffing and I said, "I smell gas too, Tom." We looked down the hill and there was another well below them some yards off.

"No wonder they aren't bothered by crowds," Tom chuckled. "It's a wonder the gas well owners don't toss them out."
"Let's get the hell outa here before we get blown up."

We hustled Stan out as politely as we could and retreated.

Earlier trips up there, we'd hit some decent caddis hatches, and once, when the water was extremely high, we saw a "blanket hatch" of Hendricksons. No rises, as the water was too high and wild.

A trip I made with Reed to fish their green drake hatch, I was flustered as the drakes there were much smaller than on Penn's. After butchering some of my best ties, I finally got several. I had a lot of tying to do that winter, to get a new supply for local fishing.

We tried the Delaware River several times, mostly in the area of Hancock, NY, with good success the first time, but it dropped off suddenly after that. That first trip, I was alone, after Dave, from town, got me all fired up about it. At home the March browns were on and the fishing was good until all the rain made the streams unfishable. A friend from

Lancaster was on the other side of Penn's one day, and suggested going to the Delaware. I had time just then, but money was low.

"No worry, just bring food. I know a place we can camp."

Thinking of the Jones brothers, I was a bit concerned, but since my sweetie was away, I went.

I was worrying the whole way there about the water levels; every stream was out of its banks. Fortunately, the Delaware had dams controlling the water. I located the area I was told about, and had a good day's and evening's fishing with dries. Blue winged olives were on but I shouldn't have worried.

As long as the fly had wings, the trout ate them, if the fly was presented right.

I met my friend later and he led me along a major railroad line to a spot under the trees. We both slept in the back of our pick-ups. Except for the trains coming by all night, and the rain making it seem like I was in a steel drum, it was all right. Just before I met my friend, I was in the river waist deep, after dark and about ready to quit, when I heard a *plunk* just up from me. I twisted around and a canoe was about to hit me! I yelled at the canoer and pushed the front end away from me.

"I'm half blind and I saw you! If you can't see any better than that, then you shouldn't be alone in a canoe after dark," I yelled, upset. I did quit then, before something else would happen.

The next trip we checked in to a campground. Stan was at the desk signing in, and wondering about fly hatches, asked "Are the Hendricksons here yet?"

The man said, "I don't know, I'll check the register."

Giggling, I asked Stan to find out if the Adams and Caddis and Drakes were here too. Apparently, it wasn't a fly fishing campground. The fishing really sucked that trip, as the cities sucked so much water from the dams that the rivers were really low—screwed up the fishing in general. Wild Bill and I tried another trip again when we heard the water was controlled better, and that they had a great tricot hatch. These are really tiny flies, but can make for good fishing. As it turned out, there was a huge tricot hatch, but they let water out at the bottom, which was ice-cold for August. Also they (NY state) stocked about a million tiny rainbow trout fry. Bottom line, we tried downstream where the water was warmer also. Couldn't catch any! So, as it was very hot, we stayed at camp and tied flies on our picnic table.

Close to ours was an Airstream trailer with an A.C. on top. This knock-out, drop-dead young *beauty* came out in a very small bikini, and did a long, strenuous workout with weights and barbells. After close to an hour, Wild Bill was gasping and sweating worse than the well-conditioned girl. After a stretching and cooling off period, she decided she wanted a canoe trip. The older Mafia type, dressed in dark city clothes, ordered a younger tough dressed in a black suit, white shirt, and wing-tipped shoes to be the paddler. Talk about people that looked out of place with all the laid-back camper types. The canoe guide did take off the suitcoat and tie, anyhow. Listening to their New Jersey-and-Mediterranean mixed accents, we decided it would be a good idea not to flirt with their "honey."

Later, I mentioned these trips to that area to a friend that had been there with the Penn State gymnastic team. I don't know what they were doing there, unless there was/is a college in that area. This Bill (yes, yet another Bill) asked if I remembered the high steel bridge that crossed the Delaware River there to Hancock, NY. I did, and remembered the shallow riffle below it.

"Well," he said, "Muriel Grosfeld (formerly one of our earliest medal winners in the Olympics) was one of their coaches, and they had been drinking some beer. She decided to climb this bridge in the moonlight and do a one-handed handstand on the very top." Not the best chaperone for the kiddies.

Cicadas are an interesting, if infrequent, big fish attracting fly. I've been able to fish it some at least three different times. It's only available every seventeen years for each brood. Different broods come in different years in different areas. I've seen it on the Juniata River when it wasn't available on the trout streams I fished. The first time I had a ball with them, but only one day. I can't recall why I only got one try that year. At that time I was fishing live bait with a fly rod and mono line. This is fine with some splitshot to bounce along the bottom, but these big bugs were being slaughtered on top. I removed all weight and after collecting some live cicadas, I was able to cast them, but not far. The trout gobbled them and I located a good feeding fish and wondered why I couldn't get the black and orange bug to him. I looked closer, and the bait was flying around in the air with my line trailing like a spider web. I learned a bit, and took a wing off before casting. That worked, but it worked better when the bug made more commotion in the water. This was in Kish Creek in an unstocked area which we knew held good fish. I killed several and one looked like a balloon, it was so stuffed. Curious, I checked its stomach and throat and counted thirty-four cicadas. I could tell the mashed ones by their bright orange eyes. This trout wasn't quite thirteen inches yet, but he was trying to be.

I saw cicadas all over the Juniata and had heard of some people having a ball with bass and carp, in other years. When I saw them, there had been hard rain and the river was high and dirty. I didn't see one fish feeding on top.

I did catch one of my largest trout on Penn's on a live cicada one year. Wild Bill and I couldn't get a bigger one in the same area. The next-to-last time they were on Penn's was fun. We tied some bad imitations that worked well enough, but not always. I believe the fish would get so stuffed, they just took some breaks to let the food settle. I remember one 15-16" trout that kept refusing my fly. I fished for others and came back an hour later. First cast and *bam!* I can't fully explain it, but it's kind of like green drake fishing, only in the daylight.

Just recently the cicadas visited our area again, but as I now have a muscle problem in my legs, I couldn't safely wade much or travel far. I did get to Penn's and tried briefly. I was rewarded by a splashy refusal on the first cast. Casting my fly, a very large imitation, it looked to me just the right size and color, but no luck in likely places, even where there were rises. I changed to a similar but much smaller fly. My first cast was caught by a gust of wind and landed ten feet away from the current in a dead backwater. Naturally a nice fat brown of 16" jumped on it and made me a happy cripple.

Overall, people didn't do as well on Penn's Creek that year as Kish and Honey Creek. The fish weren't as big at Kish and Honey Creek, but very willing. If I can just get in shape for the next brood of cicadas for our area, I'll be ready. And in my early 90's.

I've been lucky enough in my time to be on the stream during some great hatches. Maybe it's more because of my persistence, but also, I was lucky enough to have the best wife a fisherman could have. Rosalie would see me moping around when I had most of the important chores done around the house, and would tell me to "Get out and go fishing. You're getting on my nerves!" So reluctantly, I'd go, just to please my sweetie pie.

Back when I was an ironworker, we couldn't get on the steel when it was raining, too dangerous! So what was left but to go fishing? Throughout the years, I noticed that when it was raining, I'd have more success. When I began to fish flies, I noticed there were also more fly hatches, and fewer fishermen on the water. What more could a fly fisher want, as long as he or she didn't mind carrying or wearing proper foul weather gear? I've seen heavy emergences of different caddis, Hendricksons, black quills, different sulfur types, March browns, stonema, (cahills) green drakes, isonychias, and especially the blue winged olive hatches. It seemed to me that the caddis didn't care whether the sun was out or not, but most of the mayflies, I think, felt more secure when it was raining. The hard downpours were not so good; the cool drizzly type rains were best. The fish were not usually as spooky, but the natural flies could not dry their wings as fast and were on the water longer, and therefore easier targets for the trout, which made the fly fisher happier, because there were more targets for them.

Although, in my opinion, the rainy day hatches were more dense, on sunny days the emergence was more sporadic, but may have lasted longer. This is fun for the fair weather fishers, but I think the fish, in general, are harder to catch. If the fish are rising and feeding on top, there is no downside.

After a really hot, dry spell, I've always tried to be available to get stream-side if a rain looks probable. Several of my very best dry fly days were at this special type of situation. My most memorable was a day when I got on Penn's early on a July day and worked my way down to Broadwater. Zip-zero. It was as if every trout in Penn's went to live elsewhere. The water was like a dead, sterile place. Bored, I got my little fine mesh net out and waded to the water where the main flow entered the pool, and checked for bugs. Usually, nothing, then an ant, then a beetle, a dead spent wing from the evening before. This went on for 25 minutes. It was 11:30 AM and I lifted the net and there was a size 16 blue winged olive, soon another, then three more. I felt a light drizzle on my neck and gazed at the pool below me. A rise! Then another! I got my eye level with the water and looked up stream. Thousands of dark, oversized wings (for mayflies) appeared like a mini armada. I've seen this before, but not so sudden or massive. Running to shore on slippery rocks, I rigged my rod in a panic, with my pattern for a #16 blue winged olive. Soon I was catching trout. Fish were rising everywhere and not another soul was on the creek. Of course, it was July 10th and very hot. Who would be out cooking in waders in this weather except some nut? As nice as the drizzle felt to me, it must have felt great to the trout, with the bonus of trout candy floating overhead.

At certain pockets there were as many as six fish rising on the same drift as my fly. I wasn't catching as many fish as I thought I should be, so I decided to cast to one feeding fish at a time. Haste makes waste, and I could only catch one fish at a time, so my new strategy helped a lot. I was getting giddy, giggling to myself, and even smiling when I pulled the fly away unwittingly, when they were due to engulf it. After spending about half an hour trying to catch a 16-17" brown trout, I finally hooked him for about ten seconds and then he was off.

Gradually, I went to faster flowing water and could fool more, as they didn't have as much time to decide if it was real. As I worked my way back up stream, covering about two hundred yards, I began to realize how tired I was. Looking at my watch, I was shocked to see it was after 8PM. Still chuckling at my good luck at being on the stream just then, and realizing what to do, and having the right fly, and the best fishing I ever had or expect to have, I took my rod apart, fired up a cigar, and sat on the bank. After nine hours, the hatch was still going full throttle, and the fish were still feeding. I just sat there and enjoyed the spectacle. God is good.

This situation of long dry spells in warm weather doesn't always bring on a hatch of flies, but the sudden rain does usually get the trout active. One time, it was hot and muggy, and Rosalie noticed that I was getting itchy when a heavy rain was approaching.

"You're not going out now, are you? It's going to pour soon," she said.

"That's why I'm going," I replied, "but I'm just going to fish nearby in Kish Creek at a section I've never tried before and there's trout to be caught."

"Sometimes I wonder about you," she said, rolling her eyes.

"You knew I was crazy when you married me," I teased. "That's why you love me."

I parked at a nearby park and walked down a walking path about three hundred yards just as the rain started. I had no flies on, so I started fishing nymphs. I caught a few stocked fish as I walked back up the creek, then a few fall fish until I reached a spot where Kish Creek narrows to a fast chute. By then the rain was really pelting down. I began catching some wild browns then, as it rained the hardest, and some were decent trout, especially one in the 15" range that threw my fly back at me as if to say, "Ouch! That hurts!" He cleared the water by three feet. It was wild for a short while in that narrow stretch. I got a few more past a limestone cliff bend in the stream. Then the shower stopped and the sun came out, and it was like a switch turned the fish off. Even though I went upstream and fished some nice water, there was no more action. I proved my point to myself anyhow, and had fun doing it.

It certainly doesn't work all the time, but enough to make me carry rain gear if the weather threatens. One day on Penn's it happened again with a quick rain, after fishing a "green weenie" for half an hour with absolutely no action. As it was muggy out, I reluctantly put on my rain jacket and kept the same fly on that I had no luck with earlier. After I walked to a fresh set of fast water pockets, I cast to pool after pool, and the trout wouldn't even let the "weenie" settle to the bottom. It was fun, and fast, but again, as soon as the rain stopped and the sun came out, the action was over.

I thought I was pretty good at predicting the annual grannom hatch several years ago and was telling several friends about it.

"The hatch always starts about now and it's past due. It always starts in the morning between 8:30 and 9:20AM!" I said. "I've been on Broadwater two days ina row now, and it hasn't started yet. Not one caddis."

"OK," they said, appeasing me, "We'll go with you tomorrow since you guarantee us it'll definitely appear on schedule. Also because we've never seen the beginning of it."

I was lucky to see this two other years and I thought I was finally beginning to understand caddis flies, which had always confused me more than other flies as far as predicting anything.

We arrived at Broadwater a short time after 8AM and rigged our rods with an imitation and poured some coffee from our thermos and waited. And waited! And waited! There was a cool fog over the water that morning, and Jon and Big Walt were beginning to abuse me pretty much verbally. The time passed 9:30 and the abuse got worse. Ten o'clock came and passed. Ignoring them, I sat on the bank staring at the surface. Then at 10:20, I saw a fly emerge. *Never* said a word until I saw a dozen more.

Cocky-like, I said, "If you guys don't wake up, you'll miss the big hatch." I didn't say it would be daylight savings time!

By then, not hundreds, but thousands of size 14 caddis were all over the surface of Penn's, skittering, jumping up and down, flying away. My abusive friends gawked with their mouths open at the show, trying not to show they were impressed.

"The Old Master was right again," I blustered, relieved. "However, I didn't guarantee the fish would eat them."

After two hours there were only a few fish rising. They each got one on dry, and I lost one. We tried nymphs, emergers, wets, and obviously the fish were feeding with all these flies, on the water and under the water. Maybe they were full, maybe the water was cold, maybe the moon wasn't in the right phase. We had all the old excuses, but we didn't have the answers.

There's another caddis hatch that can be fun that arrives several weeks later. It's a size 16 tan with olive body, or all tan. I don't see it every year, but some years it can be great. I noticed that these caddis don't fly off the water usually, but swim or skittle to the shore line, and that really gets some splashy rises.

I had Big Walt with me in a deep, swift, tricky run that we knew held nice fish. Walt doesn't know the bugs or hatches well, but he sure knows the mechanics of presenting a dry fly. While I was pretty proud of getting a 15" and a smaller one, Walt proceeded to get three 15" browns out of that small run on his #16 dry flies. I don't remember if we got others at other spots or not, but I know we didn't top the action at that first spot. Not bad for a short evening's fishing after work.

Sometimes, when that caddis hatch is active, prospecting with nymphs, I put a dropper of a #16 bead head light olive with several turns of peacock at the head. This has done well at times.

One year this hatch was bringing fish up pretty good and I ended up in Broadwater. I was on the White Mountain side and a pair of brothers, who were both professors at West Virginia University, were across from me. We were all catching some fish and the action was getting better by the minute. At the peak of the hatch, a flock of resident wild geese flew in and landed all over the pool and proceeded to eat as many of the caddis as they could, even to the point of taking them away from the trout that weren't spooked by them yet. After trying fruitlessly to find trout still feeding, the three of us reeled in our flies and just watched. The geese gobbled most of the flies, then decided to preen themselves, splashing and ignoring us, and just had a helluva good time.

Disgusted, I said to the two brothers, "You know, they have Trout Unlimited, Pheasants Forever, The Wild Turkey Federation, and Ducks Unlimited. A friend of mine wants to start a new organization, 'Ducks and Geese Somewhat More Limited Than They Are.'"
In unison the brothers yelled back, "We'd like to be charter members!" I love the way fly fishers think.

Stopping in Madisonburg one morning at an Amish bakery (now out of business,) Stanley and I bought and gobbled sticky buns, homemade chocolate covered cherries, and some homemade root beer. We were just exploring that day and went over the mountain pass and fished Fishing Creek, briefly as there was a weed problem at that time from the upper fish hatchery. On to Spring Creek in the Bellefonte area, where, having got off to a bad start, it got worse as the wind picked up and blew my leader into dead tree branches. Stan tried to keep from laughing—but not too hard—especially when the branch broke with the wind and the current took it down the creek. I finally caught up to the mess and, unable to untangle it all, I snipped part of the leader off and rebuilt it. Deciding to put a nymph on, I tied a "Walt's worm" on, which imitates a crane fly nymph. It was a simple tie, which was good, the way my day was going. Looking up the creek, Stan was not in sight, and that was in my favor too. Regrouping,

I decided to walk down a ways and fish up. By-passing some nice water, I then fished up. The trout loved Walt's worm, (named after Walt Young) and I was having a ball hooking one fish after another in this first double run. About that time, I heard this female voice just in back of me. Startled, I turned around and this gorgeous young lady said she saw me catching all these fish (actually maybe 4 or 5) and wanted to know all about it. I tried to explain to this non-fisher-type, and asked her if she lived in the house just back of me.

"Oh no," she said, "I live up there." She pointed to a house a good city block away. I was amazed this good-looking, well built girl (the bulky sweater did not hide all of her) would travel that far to find all about fishing. I even caught a trout while I was giving her a short course on angling. We talked awhile more, then each of us went on our ways.

Later, when Stan and I met up, I gave him the whole story, including the fishing.

"When will you ever stop lying?" he said.

I answered, "You're just mad because you're not a chick magnet and don't know how to fish good!" I don't know if he ever did believe me, and I don't really care.

I see women on the stream more and more and most have a good sense for fly fishing. On Penn's one evening, at the spring hole, I was having a hard time fooling several rising fish. A couple from Canada, that were teaching at Pitt, were fishing on the other side of the island in back of me. Talking to them earlier, I realized she knew how to fish. I went over a few steps and said, "I have a couple tough fish over here I can't fool. If you guys care to try for them, you won't be crowding me."

They came over shortly and while the husband and I sat on a log, the young woman went down and caught the tough fish when I told her where they were located. It only took her several casts.

At Aumiller Flat one year I was coming down fishing a stone nymph and only got a couple. On the other side were six rough type kids in their 20's, from West Virginia. Most didn't seem to be fishing, but the one big, attractive girl was. After telling the others to "Keep the hell out till I'm done," she emerged from the brush (probably from a potty break) and proceeded to catch several trout in short order. I asked what she was using and when she said "Stone nymphs," I decided to fish elsewhere, as she was taking care of that area. She was not one to mess with.

While I'm on the subject I must tell a story about a friend I sometimes fish with, also named Denny. When he was a bachelor he lived a few doors down from me. He tried to romance all the women in the state. I came home from work one day and Rosalie said she had this strange phone call. This man called and said, "Is this where Denny lives?"

"Of course," she said, "yes, this is his wife."

The man, all flustered, said, "Well, your Denny has been fooling around with my wife!"

Thinking it was one of my friends playing a joke, Rosalie got into one of her laughing fits, and the man got so angry he hung up. After figuring out what it was all about, I was half peeved.

"The least you could have done, Rosalie, was to have been a little bit suspicious of me."

That started her laughing again, which made me grin.

She said, "If I don't know you by now, I'll never know you."

I never played poker with her.

Walt and I were fishing unsuccessfully one day at the Clay Bank Hole. I'd already broken my rod down and was in sweat pants as we carried our packs down, to save a long walk in the heat in waders. Walt was messing with an occasional riser in a back eddy that often flustered us.

I heard steps in the woods in back of me and here came two young ladies. (Not teens, but maybe in their thirties.) Both were wearing shorts and tees and sneakers, out for a walk on the old RR bed that parallels the stream There was no definite path from up there and you couldn't see the water from the trail, but they said they just wanted to get to the water. They were friendly and we talked and explained about the fishing and the area. While Walt got his waders off, put his hiking shoes on, and took his fly rod apart, the one girl wandered off and soon let out a scream. I went over and she gasped, "Snake!" Sure enough, there was a big, non-poisonous snake, with some rings around it. I know rattlesnakes and copperheads, and don't worry about the rest. We went back to the mossy bank and talked some more. I was very aware that the one was not wearing a bra, and Walt was aware of the cute redhead. Regardless, Walt and I decided to put our packs on and head for the truck. Both of us being happily married men, we still discussed the episode. Was the opportunity there? Maybe, but we weren't about to try and find out.

It's hell being a chick magnet with a conscience.

I had some friends with a camp near the old RR tunnel. Bobby was telling me about the one guy that came to their camp and was a fanatical fly fisher. A career Army man, he often spent most of his leave time at camp, and fished hard and drank some beer. He was convinced that the Clay Bank Hole, which was a deep and remote, but small pool, had a monster trout in it. Bobby and I both love a bit of devilment and love to play with people's minds a bit.

He told me that Zack once acquired a cage of white mice and tied several deer hair mice on big hooks, with this theory to chum the big monster trout. The tale goes that Zack went to the Clay Bank Hole in the wee hours, and once situated with the cage of white lab mice, reached in the cage and flipped a mouse out into the current at the head of the hole. The little mouse struggled until it got downstream in the riffles. Again Zack threw another little mouse out and it drifted down with no results. The third mouse was plopped at the edge of the current, swimming and struggling until nearing the end of the pool, there was a large swirl and a gulping splash. All excited, Zack reached for another mouse, but the cage door was open and all the mice were gone.

I told Bobby I knew who he was but didn't think he knew our connection. Eventually we'll get him. A year later on Broadwater, it was pitch dark and several of us were talking fishing. After the spinner fall was over and Zack joined us, we exchanged a few fish stories and I said, "Zack, I think I've seen you fish the Clay Bank area a lot. Don't you?"

"Yeah," he said. "It's just down the trail a ways from the shanty and I like that area."

"I know this sounds weird and all," I continued, "but tell me if I'm crazy or just imagining things. Twice now, I think I've stumbled onto a colony of wild white mice there. Have you ever seen any?"

"Who the hell were you talking to?!" Zack said, knowing he had been had.

I couldn't keep from laughing and didn't ask him if he ever caught a monster there on a white deer hair mouse pattern.

Years back, when you could camp just about anywhere, a fellow from Lancaster, who I heard is now in Montana building cane rods for a living, would camp near our parking area. He once brought a non-fishing friend along that was new to any kind of wilderness. He just loved it and had a fire going every evening and most of the day. I don't know if he ate anything else, but I saw him bake one potato after another, slather it with butter, add salt and pepper, and gulp it down. They're good, but he ate a lot of them. The fisher-camper and I would talk fishing and the newcomer would listen in awe and believe most of it.

One afternoon the camper and I were talking about nymph fishing and how many we caught that way. The new woodsman believed it all and decided he wanted to learn to fish nymphs. The camper said, tongue-in-cheek, "Show him how; you're the best I ever saw at it." (He never saw me catch one trout on a nymph.)

"Come on, Joe, I'll at least show you the basics." Down over the hill we went, straight to the stream. I was already rigged with a stone nymph, one split shot, and a strike indicator. I showed him how everything was rigged, told about different flies he could use, and led him to a nice small pocket below a pile of rocks. I narrated as I demonstrated, saying, "I'll cast into the riffles flowing into the run, like this, let it drift into the pocket, like this, then when the indicator stops, like that, I'll tighten, like this," and as if on cue, a 13" brown trout jumped out of the water and after a brief tussle, I landed and released it.

"See how easy it is?" I said, before heading back up the hill trying to keep a straight face. He was still staring at the pocket when I looked back. I never told him it's never that easy.

Not too long ago, maybe 6 or 8 years ago, me, Danny (about 40) and Nathan, then a tall, lanky teenager, were looking for a spot to watch for rising fish. We were all lazy and joking around. What a trio! Me, over 70; Danny, shorter than I, and a good fisherman, tier, and cane rod builder, but an ornery, carefree bachelor; and Nathan, 17, smart and serious but with a good sense of humor—which he needed, traveling with us.

It was hot and there were lots of fishermen, so we parked under some branches in the shade on some grass. Dan smoking cigarettes, me with a small cigar, we were just yakking, telling of different episodes we all had, when I saw a rise a cast away from shore. I told them, and only me, the blind guy, saw it. "You saw it, you get it," Danny said. "Only do it paraplegic style." Only Nathan the innocent, said, "What's that style?"

I showed him, sliding along the ground on my butt to the shore. I had to figure out how to cast with all the branches around. It wasn't legal, this "style," to wade out to where I could cast easily, so I false casted up and down over the water. The trout was in low water where one doesn't normally see a rise, but he was under a big flat rock in an easy drift, tight to the rock. I couldn't reach him on the first cast so I stripped more line out and building up line speed, shot the line above the rock. A surprisingly nice brown came up and sucked it down. I set the hook from my awkward position and the trout made a fast short run and threw the fly back to me. First there was a cheer, then the boo-birds, then we all broke up and giggled like a bunch of teenage girls. It's not necessary to have a great, successful day on the stream if you have good company, folks. This is why I keep coming back.

I go on and on about great hatches and some of the super fishing I get into from time to time, but the truth of the matter is, my bread and butter of fishing success comes from nymphing and the spinner falls, or egg-laying time for the bugs.

Nymphing can be as addictive as dry fly fishing. In fact I know many young fellows that do little else. It sounds very mysterious to the dry fly purist, and also like a lot of work—which it can be. However, the mystery can be quickly overcome by learning the basics and using standard successful flies such as a stone nymph, hare's ear, pheasant tail, or several others, and get a pal that nymphs to show you how to rig them. Then it's a matter of casting upstream and letting your line bounce down the current as naturally as you can, and every time your line stops, tighten. Usually it's a snag or rock, but often enough it's a trout.

When you gain a bit of confidence from the spongy feel when you hook a trout, you get hooked yourself. Just try to get a natural drift like a dry fly, only it's underwater and you can't see it. Think of it like Ginger Rogers said about dancing with Fred Astaire. She said, "I'm doing the same steps as Fred, but I'm doing it backwards. Why does he get all the credit?"

Many of the pros say not to use a strike indicator, but I need all the help I can get. Even though I don't need the indicator to detect strikes all the time, I do use it as "drift indicator" which helps me get a more natural drift, which in turn helps me catch more trout. When I get so good the trout need a handicap, then I'll take my indicator off.

If I ever got very good at any phase of fly fishing, it would have to be learning more about the spinner falls or egg-laying phase. This is because for most of my working years, I couldn't get on the water until evening when many of the hatches were over. However, the mayflies, once they were out of the water and into our world, have to mate, fertilize eggs, and drop their eggs into the water to start their cycles all over again.

That stage of flies which we call spinners have different traits, but on larger streams such as Penn's Creek, it usually starts later in the day, because the larger streams stay warm longer. Most mayflies still have pretty similar habits, but caddis are still a mystery to me and probably always will be.

The red quills (Hendricksons) are usually earlier as the weather is cooler then. But the different types of sulfurs and cahills are usually later, but quite dense and often after dark. The different types are *on* the water at the same time then, and if the trout get honed in on one kind, the fisherman has a real problem. Also, there are so many bugs on the water that your artificial fly is lost in the crowd. What to do? That's your problem—or your pleasure—to figure it out. To add to the problem, there's often emergences of smaller flies mixing among the spinners. It's like fishing the ever popular green drake hatch, only with much smaller flies. These are the problems the truly dedicated fly fisher loves.

Oh—one more thing. Try to have the right fly on your leader before dark, unless you're good at tying on flies with a flashlight and losing your night vision.

Well, enough on teaching and "how to." Learn on your own. It's slower, but more fun.

CHAPTER THIRTEEN— RAMBLING ON

I've met many great people over the years on the water. Long ago, sitting on a bank at Broadwater, waiting on a hatch, I'd trade stories with different folks. A surgeon, Dr. Thompson I believe, from Clearfield, was one. We'd talk flies, theories and so forth, and he just loved it there. I don't know what became of him after several years, but he never came back. He didn't care if I was a mailman and he was a surgeon. He just knew we were both fishermen and loved the area.

The same spot on the bank I shared with "Ohio," a fellow that tried to get to Penn's several times a year. To him I was "the mailman" and he was "Ohio" to me. He had the neatest fly box I ever saw, with beautiful flies all arranged by size and pattern and colors. Then I'd show him mine with the beat up flies all in a jumble and the "file 13's" that I never threw away because I might need them someday.

There was the UPS man I originally met on Fishing Creek one spring day when I lucked into a pod of "stockies" with an obscure nymph called Cate's Turkey. He also called me "the mailman" and to me he was "the Cigar Man" because he'd always give me his latest favorite cigar.

Then there was "Cocky," the big roofer that ran the Lycans Valley camp. One night, when he was ready to quit, he loudly told everyone on Broadwater it was time to quit. Since I was on the opposite side of the creek, I yelled back, "I'll quit when I feel like it, not when you're ready." I'm glad he had gimpy legs and a bad memory, because he never caught me when I was on his side of Penn's. We actually got to be good friends later on and would often trade stories across the creek. He also knew a good horseshoe pitcher I knew through tournaments, even though we lived miles apart. I think I impressed him one day when we were talking back and forth. He had just finished with a nice deep run and I asked if he minded if I tried it.

"No, go ahead," said Cocky. "I'm done with it."

I waded as far as I could and drifted a big stone nymph through, and shortly got a hefty 15" brown.

"That's a nice one," he said.

"Thanks, Cocky. I got lucky I guess." I released it.

At that time we both fished floating ants a lot in Broadwater for occasional rising trout with fair success. That was when the "McMurray Ant" was popular. It had a balsa wood body and the two sections were joined together by a short piece of mono in each part, glued with super glue and black enamel. It was a pain to make and later they came out with easy-to-tie foam, so even though the McMurray worked better, I went to foam. Poor ol' Cocky's health went bad and he's now on the other side.

Bill, the camp owner, is a neighbor from town, and I enjoy fishing with him. He's laid back and usually only fishes near camp. Not lazy, he just doesn't like to go to Broadwater. He calls it "the Fish Pond." It took a while, but finally I got him fishing artificial nymphs instead of live ones. He always did enjoy dry flies.

There was the eye doctor from Kane that I befriended one rainy day when he was staying in his car overnight. Yet another Bill, he was a meek type and I brought him back to camp and he provided a ham and I cooked fried taters and onions and green beans. After we ate and had coffee, I looked at my watch and said, "I gotta go, Bill. I have to work tomorrow. Just lock up and turn off the lights when you leave tomorrow. It was pouring rain yet.

His jaw dropped and he said, "You hardly know me and you're leaving me at your cabin?"

"Bill, if I don't trust you after fishing with you and talking with you several hours, I'll never know you."

We got together several times after that. He brought a podiatrist, Stan, with him later and I got them started fishing nymphs, and they did well. I didn't care as much for Stan as he was a bit pushy, but he was still a good guy.

Then there was Jon Sheetz, an undertaker, an appropriate name for his trade. (There was also Grubb's Diner, Wilt the florist, Heeters plumbing and heating, and Shear, the barber.) One of Jon's cohorts, Joe, was a good, if quiet, fisherman. On Broadwater one day, as the rest of us sat on the bank talking and waiting for fish to rise, Joe worked his way past us and caught 5 or 6 trout. He was slowly working a plain grub type nymph back deep. I never figured that out, as myself and another of that crew tried the same thing with no luck. Another of their gang had me entered in his log book as "the leprechaun." I laughed and asked why. He said, "Well, you're not there, and suddenly you're there." I laughed again, but what happened was, as I headed down or up stream in back of him, he was engrossed in fishing, and the water was making some noise. I came right in back of him close and said loudly, "Catching any?"

Besides, he's pretty intense anyhow.

Ol' Austin was a good ol' boy. The women loved him, and he loved guns, boats, cars, motorcycles, and fishing. For years he had a small car repair shop with inspection area which had a room in back where he sometimes lived. Never a heavy drinker, he may have strayed sometimes and his wife got tired of it and they either got divorced or separated. What was he thinking? His wife at one time was in charge of the fly tying division of Phillip's Lures. That's where Joe Brooks, Ted Trueblood, and many other fishing celebrities of the time bought their flies. Anyhow, a fence was installed between the house where his wife still lives and his garage/ sometimes bachelor pad. I remember him when he was still in his eighties, driving his big Honda cycle with his girlfriend on the tandem seat. As his health went south, he was talking to me one day, feeling a bit regretful of his past life.

"Denny, I was totaling up the other day all the money I spent on guns, boats, cycles, women, booze, fishing gear, gambling, and such. It came to $350,000 or more."

"Yeah, and the rest you just wasted."

He didn't consider it all that funny, but I just had to jump on a good opening like that.

Now I'll give an opinion of some of the writers and/or celebrities in the fly fishing world. I've met some and just knew of others. Some are on the other side now, and most don't care what I think. Wild Bill and I used to go to all the Trout Unlimited banquets and such that we could. Both of us won some nice prizes because there weren't as many big spenders then for the raffles. I won rods, reels, shadow boxes, and flies, and so did Bill, with a minimum investment on our parts.

One state banquet at the Nittany Lion Inn, the main speaker was Arnold Gingrich. He was droning on and on about a book on other fishing books that he wrote going all the way back to the Middle Ages. Bill and I were trying hard not to doze off by gazing at this beautiful, well dressed young lady a few tables away from us. Her head was wavering a bit, and during a speaker's pause *Clunk!!* her head hit the table hard as sleep claimed her briefly. It was all Bill and I could do to keep a straight face. The young lady recovered well, rubbing her elbow as if that was the problem.

Dr Bus (Alvin?) Grove was maybe the most relaxed speaker we've had, but Wild Bill and I remember one day at the parking lot on Kettle Creek when he backed longways over a borrowed graphite fly from a nearby shop at Crossforks. Bill and I were tying flies and screamed at him before he ran over the reel. Amazingly, there wasn't a mark on the rod.

Vince Marinaro was a good speaker, talented, but just loved to pat himself on the back. He never thought he got enough credit for his accomplishments. One day my friend Reed (my hero and mentor) and I were fishing the tricot hatch at Falling Springs and at lunchtime all were sitting around gabbing. Vince was going on and on about using only natural materials for flies, no synthetics blah blah blah. Reed, normally a quiet gentleman, couldn't swallow any more and asked Vince if he used bone hooks or that new-fangled Swedish steel. That shut him up for awhile. He usually had a few disciples following him around and admiring his fishing skills—and he was good.

Ed Koch had a fly shop on Yellow Breeches at Boiling Springs, and Wild Bill and I camped in back of my pickup beside the shop one night. We tied flies by propane light until it got too hot and buggy. We didn't know Ed was trying to raise chickens near us for the feathers. Really early, the roosters started crowing and there was no more sleep. I would have cursed those roosters but Bill took care of that for me. Ed had written a book on tricots and midges. One day, again at Falling Springs, on the tricot hatch, he had some disciples following him around. As they passed Bill, Ed said, (remembering us) "You won't hook him—he teases everyone that tries for him." Bill promptly hooked and landed him in front of Ed and his crew. Never at a loss for words, Bill said, "That S.O.B. never had me try for him."

Charlie Fox was a dandy fellow. We first met him below his house at the LeTort doing stream improvement with a shovel and wheelbarrow. We knew he wrote a book on warm water fishing and lures. He got all excited telling us about his homemade muskie lure. Knowing Bill and I were going to a seminar at Fisherman's Paradise soon, on Spring Creek, and he would be there, he promised to bring his lure.

The seminar came and we talked to Charlie about his lure while there was a casting demo going on.

"Let's don't talk about that here; these people don't understand that kind of fishing."

So he led us back to his little blue VW Beetle and opened the hood, which was his trunk. "Oh darn, I didn't put that lure in." But he showed us his split bamboo casting rod that he made (or salvaged from a fly rod.) I think he liked to make all his own gear.

Bill and I took "Buck" Metz, a local guy from Belleville that also did business with Bill, of Metz Necks, now part of Umpqua feathers, to the Limestone Valhalla one day, and showed him Falling Springs, Big Spring at Newville, and stopped at the LeTort at Charlie Fox's meadow to eat some fast food. Buck was in the middle and Bill and I on the outside. Buck was just getting started in the feather business, prompted by Dr. George Harvey, whose fishing and fly tying courses he'd taken at Penn State. Buck was studying genetics for his family business, a large chicken hatchery. Dr. Harvey talked Buck into perfecting the quality of dry fly necks, which he did shortly. Anyhow, I winked at Wild Bill when we finished our lunch, and we heaved our trash out the window onto the hallowed ground. I thought Buck would have a heart attack. When he recovered, we picked it up, and looked over the LeTort. Later that day we fished the Yellow Breeches at Allenberry Play House and Resort.

George Harvey probably got more people tying flies and fly fishing than anyone in the world. I had a chat with him in a mall several years ago in State College while he was waiting for his housekeeper. He was in his 90's then and still sharp as a tack. Joe Humphries took over when George retired. Joe is still very active and spreading the gospel of fishing and making money doing it. He was a wrestling coach at an area high school and later, at Penn State, before he and Dr. Harvey became friends.

Greg Hoover, an entomologist at Penn State, a good friend, partnered in a book with another writer, and was very disillusioned by the experience. He's very talented himself and needs to do his own book.

I won a great prize at a banquet in Carlisle one year: a shadow box by Poul Jorgenson. It had a lithograph print of a brown trout and six traditional flies, plus six cutwing versions of the same patterns. Poul did the whole thing himself. He learned from William Blades, and every fly he tied was perfect. I met him different times, and what a gentleman and talent. I believe he made presentation salmon flies in the Baltimore area for a few years also. He was from Denmark, and in my opinion, the best fly tier ever.

Ernest Sweibert was a "boy wonder" who also learned to tie from William Blades fly tying school. Ernie tied on TV as a young man. Multi-talented, he was not only a prolific writer of angling books, but also painted the flies in his books. He did a survey for Argentina for their park system in lower Patagonia and Andes regions, an sampled the streams long before it became a destination of fly fishing yuppies. A world traveler (his family must have been well-to-do), he fished South America, salmon in Norway, and all over the American West. I never met the man, but I know people that did. A classmate went to school at Ohio State with him and later they were next-door neighbors with him at Princeton, NJ. My niece typed an article for him on March browns when she was an office manager at Fly Fisherman magazine in Vermont before they moved to Stackpile books in Harrisburg, PA. He drank wine and ate cheese with Hemingway's son Jack near their home in Idaho along the stream. He yuppified fly fishing. Us rednecks barged in just because it's fun. Ernie was a pioneer for fly fishing, especially his book *Matching the Hatch*. Ernie did it all, and did it well.

William Blades was an Englishman who settled in the Midwest. He not only was a good friend of Poul Jorgenson, but his fly tying school also taught young Ernest Sweibert to tie.

Jack Hemingway was in an intelligence outfit during WWII, and when parachuting behind enemy lines in Germany, he brought a fly rod along. That's my kind of guy.

Charlie Meck is a very ambitious and prolific writer from Centre County, PA, already with multiple articles and books. He was formerly a professor at Penn State, I believe.

Walt Young was the editor of the PA Outdoor Times. I knew him as a guide at Spruce Creek and he worked at that fly shop and also Flyfisher's shop in State College. I used to think of him as a snuff-chewing hippie, but found out he is an intelligent, talented tier, great photographer, and all-around good guy.

Probably the best speaker and show for any banquet our Trout Unlimited chapter ever had. (We had yearly banquets since the 1960's. This was our main fund-raiser.) He was also the main person responsible for me trying to write at my ripe old age, with no formal training. It will probably come to naught, but it kept me from getting a bad case of cabin fever.

I tried night fishing with big wet flies after reading Jim Bashline's book on the subject. It worked pretty good sometimes, but I quit when I found out how hard it was to revive the hefty browns when the warm waters of August wore them out after a hook-up. I had met Jim earlier when I was working at Aberdeen Proving grounds and he was at the Baltimore Sun. He knew Earl Ashenfelter, who was my boss. Earl was an expert on the lower Susquehanna River where it empties into the Chesapeake Bay. This social was at a crab feast, and if you didn't like crabs and beer, you wouldn't like it. I took Jim to his car one night when he was our yearly banquet speaker, after our group stopped at a local tavern for a few cold ones. Because I don't drink beer, or drink much at all, I was elected to take Earl to his car where someone was to meet him on the way to town. I was a bit concerned about him getting back safely to his wife, Sylvia, at Spruce Creek, where they retired. Sylvia also wrote outdoor articles, usually recipes for game and fish. Sylvia joined Jim on the other side in September of 2011.

Another true but comical story about Vince Marinaro happened when he was camped at our parking lot at Penn's Creek. He needed something from the store but had no transportation. Lucky Vince! Wild Bill volunteered with his shiny new red Subaru. Bill was a pretty fast driver on those dusty dirt roads at that time, as many of us tended to be. Anyhow, when Bill came skidding to a halt in the parking lot on the return trip, Vince jumped out right away and said, "I'll never, *ever*, get in that 'Japanese Ferrari' again with that crazy S.O.B.!"

We all got a chuckle over that. Bill must have given him a real treat.

Finally there's Reed, who as I mentioned before, was my hero and mentor. He was the one that got me started on taking fly fishing seriously and to study the bugs more. More important, he demonstrated stream courtesy by example. A quiet, studious man, he grew up in a rough neighborhood with outdoor "outlaws"—poachers and such. He spent time in the Army as a rifle instructor, and did some wild wandering briefly. Later, he was a news director for a local radio station, and at the same time had a small tackle and outdoor shop. Quite a hunter as well as a fisherman, I knew of him killing a bear with a bow and arrow before there was an archery season. He was using a thorax tie mayfly pattern before it was introduced in Marinaro's book. He fished with all the "limestoners" on a regular basis.

Later, he became an oculist for two local industries as well as the general public. He always wanted to do things the correct way, for example, when deciding to take up biking, he bought a book on it and got a $700 bike when a $200 bike was considered expensive. Always trying to improve himself, he took college courses at age 65 and became an audiologist and sold and serviced hearing aids. Never one to sit on his laurels, he went back to school at age 75 and became a Brethren minister. He said he needed to give back, as he had received so much. Alas, along with other physical problems, he lost some of the use of his legs, which interfered with his fishing. I remember he got a float tube, but was flustered because propelling it with ping pong paddles was very difficult. Our last trip together we went to Joe McMullin's at Spruce Creek (which Donnie Beaver later bought for a big money fishery.) I went downstream awhile, and shortly after I returned, Reed took a spill on the other side. I helped him back over, and he, Joe, and I spent some good time on lawn chairs telling tales and watching some of Joe's big trout cruising. He still had a big smile on his face on the way home.

Just because my hero became a minister, that doesn't mean I'm going to preach to anyone. However, I do have some pet gripes, besides regular bad courtesy on the streams.

Mainly, I hate fishing contests. I won't publicly fight them because they're usually for the benefit of worthy causes. But I was always drawn to fishing because of the peace and tranquility of it all.

Bass Master contests are the most disgusting, with all the screaming, celebrating, and thanking God for giving them a big fish, which means more money in their pockets. Then the operators of the contests are getting rich, able to supply a slew of $30,000 to $40,000 boats with all the bells and whistles attached. These are nothing like small town contests that give *all* the profits to volunteer fire companies and other worthwhile causes. I think what turned me off most was the corporate fly fishing people, that had televised spectacles where the contestants actually *ran* from one pool to another, splashing and working themselves into a frenzy for "Team Orvis," "Team Loomis," "Team Sage," and others.

What kind of message are they trying to convey to the youth of America? Catch as many as you can at all costs, or else? We have basketball, baseball, football, all kinds of contests on TV game shows. Most of this is good: be the best you can be, at whatever you try. But where does the friendly competition stop, and the hardnosed "win at all costs" attitude take over?

Put the score card away, and just go along a pretty stream and enjoy. Try to catch some, but don't get caught up in whether you have success or not.

Have fun on the water.

PHOTO GALLERY

Cookie-eating horses along the Boulder River in Montana.

Looking upstream on Penn's Creek from Swift Run.

Upper Broadwater in the autumn.

Not all the fish we caught in British Columbia were this big.

Adult brown trout from several miles away seeking cold, oxygenated water where Swift Run enters Penn's. This was during a long hot stretch with low warm water, August 2, 1999.

The "chick magnet" in Bull River, B.C.V

THANKS

This book could not have happened without the understanding, love, and even encouragement of my best friend and wife of over fifty years, Rosalie.

Also, my daughter, Dianne Carroll, though living miles away, did all my dirty work, such as typing, editing, computer work, and contact work with the publishing team. As I'm electronically illiterate, and too stubborn to learn, she took pity on the old man.

Thanks too, to all my fishing buddies and great people I met along beautiful Penn's Creek and the other beautiful streams, rivers, lakes, and ponds.

Remember, people: there's a lot of unanswered rises out there.

Cover artwork by Steve Torok
Cover photo by Karen Beatty
Author photo by Jan Snedeker

CPSIA information can be obtained at www.ICGtesting.com
Printed in the USA
LVOW071711200212

269551LV00012B/118/P